Child Trafficking in the Indo-Myanmar Region

About the Authors

Dr. Shukhdeba Sharma Hanjabam (MSW, PhD) is Head, Department of Social Work, Indira Gandhi National Tribal University, Regional Campus, Manipur, Makhan, Kangpokpi District, Manipur. He was a Consultant (Research), for Manipur Commission for Protection of Child Rights, Imphal. He can be contacted at <hanjabam@gmail.com>.

Dr. Sapam Dilipkumar (LLM, PhD) is teaching Law at LMS Law College, DM University, Imphal. He is also the member of Juvenile Justice Board, Imphal West District, Manipur. He can be contacted at <spmdilip@gmail.com>.

Dr. Ningthoujam Rameshchandra (MSW, PhD) is ICSSR Post Doctoral Fellow at the Department of Economics, Sikkim University, Gangtok. He can be contacted at <rameshningthoujam@gmail.com>.

Child Trafficking in the Indo-Myanmar Region

A Case Study of Manipur

Shukhdeba Sharma Hanjabam
Sapam Dilipkumar
Ningthoujam Rameshchandra

CONCEPT PUBLISHING COMPANY PVT. LTD.
NEW DELHI-110059

ISBN-13: 978-93-88937-09-2

First Published 2020

Published and Printed by

Concept
Since 1974

Concept Publishing Company Pvt. Ltd.
A/15-16, Commercial Block, Mohan Garden,
New Delhi-110059 (INDIA)
T : 91 11 25351460, 91 11 25351794
E : publishing@conceptpub.com; *W* : www.conceptpub.com

Cataloging in Publication Data--Courtesy: D.K. Agencies (P) Ltd. <docinfo@dkagencies.com>

Hanjabam, Shukhdeba Sharma, 1983- **author.**
Child trafficking in the Indo-Myanmar region : a case study of Manipur / Shukhdeba Sharma Hanjabam, Sapam Dilipkumar, Ningthoujam Rameshchandra.
pages cm
Includes bibliographical references and index.
ISBN 9789388937092

1. Child trafficking—India—Manipur. 2. Child trafficking—Government policy—India—Manipur. 3. Child trafficking—Law and legislation—India—Manipur. I. Dilipkumar, Sapam, author. II. Rameshchandra, Ningthoujam, author. III. Title.

LCC HV6250.4.C48H36 2019 | DDC 364.1551 23

प्रियंक कानूनगो
Priyank Kanoongo
अध्यक्ष
Chairperson

भारत सरकार
GOVERNMENT OF INDIA
राष्ट्रीय बाल अधिकार संरक्षण आयोग
NATIONAL COMMISSION FOR PROTECTION OF CHILD RIGHTS
नई दिल्ली-110 001
New Delhi-110 001

NCPCR

Foreword

I extend my delighted greetings to Mr. Shukhdeba Sharma Hanjabam, Mr. Sapam Dilipkumar and Mr. Ningthoujam Rameshchandra Singh for their invaluable contribution and efforts in writing the book entitled "Child Trafficking in the Indo – Myanmar Region".

The book may explores the gaps and lack of synchronization in the implementation of laws and policies relating to human trafficking particularly child Trafficking. I hope that the book would enlighten those from various disciplinary backgrounds, policy makers and researchers as well as the child rights defenders and general readers alike as it throws new insight to the subject.

(Priyank Kanoongo)

29.07.2019

5वां तल, चन्द्रलोक बिल्डिंग, 36, जनपथ, नई दिल्ली-110 001
5th Floor, Chanderlok Building, 36, Janpath, New Delhi-110 001
दूरभाष/Ph: 011-23478212, 23731583 फैक्स/Fax: 011-23731584
ई-मेल/E-mail: cp.ncpcr@nic.in वेब/Web: www.ncpcr.gov.in

Preface

Human trafficking has become a serious global issue of unforeseen proportions of the twenty-first century. By its nature of exploitation, human trafficking has also been increasingly referred to as "modern-day slavery", and this has prompted rapid proliferation of international, regional, and national anti-trafficking laws, and inspired states to devotee normous financial and bureaucratic resources to its eradication. Over the last decade, the volume of human trafficking has increased though the exact numbers are not known; it is one of the most lucrative criminal trades, next to arms and drug smuggling undertaken by highly organized criminals. The reasons for increasing it, as a global phenomenon, are multiple and complex which also affects rich and poor countries alike. The popular perception of trafficking is the sexual exploitation of women and children; however, children are trafficked for a variety of reasons. There are various social, economic and political conditions, which create a situation of vulnerability specially, for women and children, who were trapped into trafficking.

The United Nations "Protocol to Prevent, Suppress and Punish Trafficking in Persons, Especially Women and Children, supplementing the United Nations Convention against Transnational Organized Crime" (otherwise known as the Palermo Protocol) adopted in 2000 has been widely and internationally accepted Convention. According to Article 3 of the UN Protocol, trafficking in persons is defined as "the recruitment, transportation, transfer, harbouring or receipt of persons, by means of the threat or use of force or other forms of coercion, of abduction, of fraud, of deception, of the abuse of power or of a position of vulnerability or of the giving or receiving of payments or benefits to achieve the consent of a person having control over another person, for the purpose of exploitation". Exploitation here shall include, at a minimum, the exploitation of the prostitution of others or other form of sexual exploitation, forced labour or services, slavery or practices similar to slavery, servitude or the removal of organs. Thus trafficking can be conceptualized in, first, the transportation of a person; second, force, fraud, or coercion; and, finally, exploitation.

UNODC (2014) reveals that most of the offenders are mostly men, while most of the detected victims are female (mainly women, but also a significant number of juvenile girls) and trans-regional trafficking accounts for nearly a quarter of all trafficking flows albeit it is less common than the domestic or intraregional types.

In Indian context, the Criminal Law (Amendment) Act, 2013 amended section 370 of the Indian Penal Code defined trafficking as whoever, for the purpose of exploitation (a) recruits, (b) transports, (c) harbours (d) transfer or (e) receives, a person or persons, by first using threat, or Secondly—using force, or any other form of coercion, or Thirdly, by abduction, or Fourthly by practicing fraud, or deception or Fifthly by abuse of power, or Sixthly by inducement, including the giving or receiving of payments or benefits, in order to achieve the consent of any person having control over the person recruited, transported, harboured, received, commits the offence of trafficking. The person who commits the offence of trafficking shall be punished with rigorous imprisonment for a term which shall not be less than seven years, but which may extend to ten years, and shall also be liable to fine.

The International Agreement for the Suppression of White Slave Traffic formed during 1904-1910 was the first of its kind to combat human trafficking in trafficking history. Thereafter, a series of legal instruments (with or without amendments of the above mentioned instrument) came into being for the criminalisation of human traffickers. Some of them are, Trafficking in Women and Children (1921), International Convention for the Suppression of the Traffic in Women of Full Age (1933), Suppression of the Traffic in Persons and of the Exploitation of the Prostitution of Others (1949), etc. These above mentioned series of instruments were either inadequate as a law to be applied or enforced and the concept is often confused with human smuggling and migration, given that these practices also involve the movement of persons albeit there are important differences between them. As a result, these above mentioned early anti-trafficking conventions were eventually consolidated into the 1949 Convention known as the Suppression of the Traffic in Persons and of the Exploitation of the Prostitution of Others, which basically referred to trafficking as a problem associated with prostitution. Thus, having started in early decades, a series of international instruments against trafficking were adopted throughout the twentieth century. Further, it adopted the Convention on the Elimination of all Form of Discrimination against Women, in 1979 with an objective to improve the situation of women in the World. Article 6 of the Convention obligates the states parties to take all appropriate measures including enactment of legislation to suppress all forms of trafficking in women and exploitation or prostitution of women.

The World Conference on Human Rights, held in Vienna in 1993, also stresses the importance of working towards the elimination of all forms of sexual harassment, exploitation and trafficking in women. India has also signed the said convention on 30th July, 1980 and ratified on 9th July, 1993. India is one of the parties to Child Right Convention, 1989 as well to the first Optional Protocol on Involvement of Children in Armed Conflict 2000 and the Second Optional Protocol on the Sale of Children, Child Prostitution and Child Pornography, 2000. She has to fulfil the international obligation by implementing the provisions of the CRC, 1989 and its optional protocols under international law and practice. India has finally ratified the UN protocol on human trafficking on 5th May, 2011, along with conventions against internationally organised crime and corruption. In fact, ratification of this convention means that it is now binding on India to develop a law that conforms to the international convention and its provisions. Nevertheless, traffickers of forced labour now come within the purview of the law in the country. Thus, the criminal gangs involved in large-scale kidnappings, abductions and forced labour of children go scot-free as the laws in the country are more biased towards prosecuting the employers or pimps in the case of prostitution.

At the regional level, the SAARC Convention on Preventing and Combating Trafficking in Women and Children was unanimously adopted by the SAARC countries on 5th January 2002 in Kathmandu. The purpose of this Convention is to promote cooperation amongst Member States so that they may effectively deal with the various aspects of prevention, interdiction and suppression of trafficking in women and children; the repatriation and rehabilitation of victims of trafficking and prevention the use of women and children in international prostitution networks, particularly where the countries of the SAARC region are the countries of origin, transit and destination.

The Constitution of India, as per the general criminal laws and special laws, prohibits and criminalises human trafficking. Article 23 of the Constitution of India prohibits trafficking in human being and other similar forms of force labour and pronounce that such acts are offences punishable in accordance with law. Article 24 of the Constitution also provides that no child, below the age of 14 years, shall be employed to work in any factory or mine or engaged in any other hazardous employment. It is further provided by the Article 37 of the Constitution that the state shall direct its policy towards securing that children are given adequate opportunities and facilities to develop in a healthy manner, so that children and the youths are protected against such exploitation. Besides IPC, the Immoral Traffic Prevention Act, 1956, Protection of Children from Sexual Offences Act, 2012, Juvenile Justice (Care and Protection of Children) Act, 2015, the draft Trafficking of Persons (Prevention, Protection, and Rehabilitation) Draft Bill, 2016 are some of the important mechanisms for combating human trafficking. On top of it, many policies are also formulated for rehabilitation and reintegration of the victim of human trafficking. So, India has now steel frame of law which can prosecute those who are involved in committing the crime of human trafficking and policies for rehabilitation and reintegration of the victim. However, India has been a source, destination and transit country for human trafficking. The Union Home Minister, Shri Rajnath Singh, while inaugurating the National Conference on Anti Human Trafficking 2015, has stated that human trafficking is a very sensitive and serious issue and termed it as a borderless organised crime. He cited that more than 1.5 lakh people (as per UN Office on Drugs and Crime) were reported as victims in a single year in South Asia. It is reported that India is the main recipient of an estimated 1,50,000 women and girls trafficked from

South Asia to feed the commercial sex industry. In addition, India is also reported to be the source and transit country for the sex trafficking of women and children from and for the Middle East. On the other hand, more than two million women and children are trapped in commercial sex work in the red-light districts of India.

Human Trafficking in North East India

The National Commission for Protection of Child Rights (NCPCR) reported that the states of Manipur, Assam, Meghalaya, Nagaland and Arunachal Pradesh were the 'source' states in the North East from where children as young as five years old were trafficked in the name of free education. The 'destination' states of these children were Tamil Nadu, Karnataka, Andhra Pradesh and Kerala. Poor parents were being lured by traffickers with high expectation of quality education for their children. In addition, lack of basic infrastructure such as road connectivity, power, hospitals, etc. and insurgency in their local areas, led parents to send their children out. More important was the role of middlemen who found it a lucrative business scouting for children from North East to the orphanages in Southern States. Most such orphanages/homes raised donations against the photographs of children sent to donors. There is no regulation on the activities of the middlemen who arrange and transport children from the North Eastern States on the pretext of free education. There is also little or no check on the illegal/unregistered Children's Homes being run in the Southern Indian States. A lack of regular inspection and surveillance by the Social Welfare/Social Defence authorities, Anti-Human Trafficking Units and local police in the districts/States where these children end up also contribute to the flourishing of these illegal activities. In addition, Trafficking in Person Report 2010, published by the United States, Department of State carried the evidence of NGO report on duping of girls from North East India with promise to provide job and then forcing them into prostitution as well as forced marriage. It is also reported that brides are also in high demand in the state of Haryana and other Northern states of India due to the low sex ratio caused by sex selective abortion.

The Department of Social Welfare, Government of Manipur

has rescued and repatriated 530 children during the period of 2008-2016 (26 June). The department has rehabilitated and reintegrated them in the society through school education and by providing vocational training. The year 2008 (October) was a landmark in Manipur while reporting the issues of human trafficking particularly children with the return of 4 girls from Tamenglong District, Manipur and one from Assam, after being trafficked to Singapore. These girls were recruited by a fake agency through its local based agents by promising jobs in Singapore. The state of affairs over the last few years is increasingly known as a source as well as a destination point for trafficking of women and children. It is a deeply entrenched and a growing phenomenon in the conflict prone areas primarily in rural neighbourhood especially the hill districts of Manipur. Many of these rescued victims are as young as seven years who left home when they were 3-4 years.

Methodology of the Study

The study aims to identify the root causes and modus operandi of child trafficking. It also aims to find out the status of child trafficking in Manipur and the initiatives taken by the state agencies. The need of the study arisen is because of the fact that Manipur in particular and North East India in general is also one of the sources, transits and destinations for women and child trafficking, especially for sexual exploitation, prostitution and child labour. The region has been a fertile ground for human trafficking for various reasons such as armed conflict, ethnic tension, lack of development and job opportunity and illiteracy. The issue of trafficking seems to be increasing despite the intervention by the government by way of constituting (i) State Level Committee to Combat Human Trafficking chaired by the Chief Secretary, Government of Manipur; (ii) Anti-Human Trafficking Units in all the districts by the state Home Department (under the guidelines of the Ministry of Home Affairs, Government of India (GoI); (iii) Anti-Trafficking Squads at the State and District level by the Department of Social Welfare, Government of Manipur; and (iv) Grant-in-Aid given to NGOs for prevention, rescue and rehabilitation of trafficking victims. For instance, MHA Anti Human Trafficking, UNODC Country Assessment report on Anti-Human Trafficking, 2013 and other available source on Child

Trafficking examined by NCPCR (2015) revealed that North East India has emerged as a high source of area for trafficking of women and children. However, there are very limited studies in trying to understand the issue through a multidisciplinary approach in Manipur except few seminars/conferences/workshops by concerned government agencies and NGOs involved in this issue. It is in this regards, the study was undertaken to analyse and examine the data compiled by the Department of Social Welfare, Government of Manipur. The study will help to anticipate ways and means to effectively combat child trafficking in Manipur. In order to respond to the objectives, the study followed the combined methodological approach of quantitative methodology supplemented by qualitative methodology. It was an exploratory research design.

The data for the study was mainly based on the official compilation of the Department of Social Welfare, Government of Manipur. There are two sets of data or rather two ways of documenting the data of child trafficking in Manipur. The first data set is a compilation of the period from 2008 to 2013 (August) with 486 reported child trafficking from 39 cases. The second data set is the compilation of the period from 2013 (23 November) – 2016 (26 June) with 80 reported child trafficking from 5 cases. Since the pattern of documentation was different, the two data sets could not be developed as one single data set for the study. So, for the purpose of the study, the first data set was used as it had the scope to examine the cases than the second data set. Besides, the number of cases in the second data set was very less as compared to the first data set. This does not mean that the first data set is perfect for the study. It has a number of limitations particularly in developing individual profiles of the traffic victims and other socio-economic parameters. Thus, the findings were presented in simple frequency tables as there is limited scope for statistical analysis. However, the study incorporates the data from the second data set, whenever it gets the opportunity. The table and figures which are developed by combining the two data sets were specifically marked 2008-2016 along with the name of the tables and figures. Besides, a note is also given to understand the tables and figures easily.

The major limitation of the study which we feel is the inability to visit the victims and their families to fill the gap in the documentation developed by the department. We did try to visit the victims and their family members but we came to know that the follow up by the department, particularly the concerned CWC, needs to be strengthened. So, we mostly concentrated on the government compiled data supplemented by the qualitative interviews. To collect data, interviews with open-ended questions was conducted with various stakeholders such as victim families, child rights based NGOs; civil society activists, government officials dealing with the issues of child, police officials, member of CWCs, JJBs and MCPCR etc. The stakeholders were indentified through purposive and snowballing sampling method. The method of saturation point will be used to discontinue the data collection process for the qualitative process.

However, it may be because of the sensitivity of the issues or may be because of its possible linkage with the conflict situation, many of the stakeholders/respondents who were consented to interview or to respond the questionnaires later declined or not responded inspite of repeated reminders by our team. Since it was a time-bound study, it was later decided to drop the respondents.

Findings

The main cause of child trafficking in Manipur is mostly due to the need for quality school education and not merely because of poverty. The mode of recruitment for child trafficking is mostly through the local agents who, almost in all cases, are members of the community or from the same villages where the victims reside. But, due to lack of factual information, it is not able to ascertain the direct involvement of these local agents. The victim were recruited by convincing their families and relatives by promising free school education and free boarding (56.4%) plus Employment (28.2%) and Skill Training (7.7%). This indicates that the trafficker seems to have studied and understand the traffic scenario of Manipur and more particularly at the local level from where they are planning to recruit children.

During the period of 2008-2016 (till June 26), 66 reported incident of child trafficking were reported throughout Manipur and in that 44 incidents are reported from the five hill districts whereas only 22 incidents are reported from the four districts of Imphal valley. The reported number of child trafficking during the period is 530 children. It was also reported that 135 children were rescued in the year 2010, which is the highest reported case of child trafficking in Manipur. But, the cases reported from the year 2011 till 2013 is a concern and also alarming as the number of cases are all above 100 except 2011. This is alarming because the situation has to be read with the background that the state mechanism to combat trafficking has already put in place particularly by the Department of Social Welfare and Department of Home, Government of Manipur. In addition, the Child Welfare Committees (CWCs) which are constituted under the JJ Act were already in operation since 2007 in all the districts of Manipur.

There are only eight incidents of trafficking in the year 2010 but it has the highest number in terms of child trafficking (135). The incidents as well as number of trafficked children for the year 2008 and 2009 were reported to be the same. But, it is observed by child activist that the year 2008 and 2009 should not be considered a good years. It may be because of the lack of documentation either with the government or with the NGOs working on issues of trafficking. Unfortunately, there was no NGO exclusively focusing on child trafficking as it was clubbed under the issue of child rights. In the year 2011, as compared to the subsequent years, the number of trafficked children is less (53), but, the number of incident is the highest (11). Majority i.e. 31 (79.5 %) of the rescued victims are reported to be from Manipur, while only 08 (20.5%) are from other states of India particularly from North East India. This may be because of the fact that the government interventions that are specific to child trafficking seem to be taking back seat.

The route for trafficking seems to be multiplied with the increasing number of trafficking incident. For instance, we have different routes to go to Guwahati from Imphal. But our concern is the change of direction. For instance, the main route for trafficking was towards Guwahati-Kolkata and finally to South Indian states particularly Tamil Nadu. But, we have noticed that the number of cases relating to trafficking of children in the name of providing quality education has been increased and distributed all-over India. It is also found that the victims of intercountry trafficking was carried out by air through Imphal-Guwahati-Kolkota and then to Singapore. In addition to Guwahati direction, now we notice that the victims are being trafficked through the Imphal–Moreh in India and towards Myanmar and finally destined to Singapore. It does not mean that, this new route is the main route of intercountry trafficking. But, there is also a possibility of using multiple routes.

In terms of rescued children, 48.7 per cent of the cases of rescued children were reported from different parts of Manipur but the majority of the cases (51.3%) were reported from outside the State of Manipur. And out of the 51.3 per cent cases reported, 28.2 per cent of the cases are reported only in South India particularly Tamil Nadu (15.4%), Karnataka (7.7%) and Kerela (5.1%). The remaining covers the different regions of India such as Eastern (West Bengal), Western (Maharashtra), Northern (Haryana), Central (Uttar Pradesh) and North Western (Rajasthan) etc. Further, Tamil Nadu with 33.3 per cent is shown as one of the favourite destinations for the trafficked children of Manipur. It is closely followed by Karnataka (7.7%) and Kerela (5.1%). It was also reported that rescue from unauthorised children home was very prominent. Tamil Nadu topped the number with 42.9 per cent of the unauthorised home followed by Karnataka (21.4%) and Rajasthan (14.3%). In terms of number of children rescued, 151 children (54.51%) were reported only from the State of Tamil Nadu.

The rescued victims, 82.1 per cent from Manipur are now repatriated and restored to their families. While 15.4 per cent of the victims particularly from outside the state of Manipur were handed to their respective Child Welfare Committees to be restored and repatriated to their respective parents and to provide the necessary facilities through their respective States. The victims were rehabilitated by providing school education (33.3%). But it is unfortunate to observe that the government is sending back the victims to the government school system of their district which they considered a failure.

The action taken against the perpetrators of the child trafficking are in the form of filing of First Information Report (FIR) with 33.3 per cent and by awarding jail term with 7.7 per cent. And in terms of the traffickers who belong to other states, it was reported that 35.9 per cent of the perpetrators were reported to have taken against them. But it is not sure what type of actions were taken against them. What we fail to identify in this study is how many of them are released on bail and how many of the cases are not able to proceed further. The table also indicates that some of the perpetrators (7.7%) of the trafficking cases could not be identified. This is mainly because there are high chances that the traffickers must have successfully convince them to come on their own way without even making them to realise that they are in the process of trafficking.

The Committees constituted by the State Government such as State Level Committee to Combat Child Trafficking headed by Chief Secretary; State Advisory Committee for Prevention and Combating Trafficking of Women and Children for Commercial Sexual Exploitation headed by the Chief Secretary; and District Level Anti-Trafficking Squad headed by Director, Department of Social Welfare, Government of India seems to have limited activities. Their activities did not even find a space of their respective departmental annual reports.

Recommendations

As the main causes of child trafficking is search for quality school education, there is the urgent need to rejuvenate the school education system in Manipur. A time bound 'Manipur School Education Commission' headed by an academician should be constituted with members drawn from various walks of life. The committee should be jointly monitored by the Manipur Commission for Protection of Child Rights and Directorate of Education (School), Government of Manipur.

As the CWCs of Manipur is in a pathetic condition, there is a need to seriously strengthen the CWCs by the government at the earliest. As a first step, they should clear the long pending dues and establish a permanent office with required support staff. Further, a study to examine the status of CWCs of Manipur, similar to that of the study undertaken by the National Commission for Protection of Child Rights should be conducted at the earliest.

As the government Committees including the high level committee remains invisible even in their respective departmental annual administrative reports, there is a need to restructure the committees, so as to create more space for members who can fully dedicate to the mandate of the committees. The involvement of government officials particularly the heads of departments, who are already overloaded with their departmental activities should be minimised.

As the process to influence the victim families and relatives was mostly done at the village level, there is an urgent need to sensitise the village level government institutions and responsible village officials including the women about the causes and consequences of child trafficking. The Manipur Commission for Protection of Child Rights should take the responsibility of the organising programme in consultation with NCPCR, Department of Social Welfare, Government of Manipur and its linking departments or stakeholders.

The stakeholders such as Department of Social Welfare, Police Department, Directorate of Education (school), Health Department, Municipal or Panchayat Authorities, District Administration, in consultation with the Manipur Commission for Protection of Child Rights and NGOs working for the promotion and protection of child rights should converse the irresponsibilities in combating child trafficking in the state of Manipur. The Department of Social Welfare could be identified as the nodal department for making effective linkage among the stakeholders.

Considering the importance of the central security forces deployed in Manipur under the Ministry of Home and Ministry of Defence, their role is pivotal in combating child trafficking as they are deployed in sensitive and border areas, where the state machinery presence is limited. Besides rescuing the victims, they can provide crucial information to the stakeholders as discussed above. For instance, there were reported cases of rescuing of child trafficking in the Indo-Myanmar region particularly Moreh by the central security forces. Thus, there is an urgent need to sensitise them particularly who are deployed in the border areas. However, for effective coordination, there is a need to set up a coordination committee for the state and central security forces in order to share information and exchange of idea for combating child trafficking.

As we have experienced that the lack of systematic documentation has weakened the data for child trafficking in Manipur, there is a need to develop an official format for documentation. This will help to document the cases in a continuous process irrespective of the capacity, commitment and creativity of the responsible person, which we feel is the practice in the state.

As the Government of Manipur is only implementing laws enacted by the Parliament and policies formulated by the Central

Government to combat child trafficking, it is recommended to formulate and adopt a State Child Policy at the earliest. Further, in order to contextualise the policy, Manipur Commission for Protection of Child Rights should invite different stakeholders (State and non-State) of the state. They should be involved in formulating the policy. A review of the existing State Plan of Action for Children adopted by the Department of Social Welfare could be the beginning in formulating the policy.

Acknowledgements

We are grateful to the Ministry of Women and Child Development, Government of India for sponsoring the study through the Manipur Commission for Protection of Child Rights, Imphal.

We are also grateful to Shri S.K. Sharma, Chairperson, Manipur Commission for Protection of Child Rights and their members for entrusting the research work to us.

We are also grateful to Shri L. Nabakishore Singh, Director, Department of Social Welfare, Government of Manipur and his concerned staff for providing the trafficking data maintained by their department.

Lastly, we are grateful to our respondents for providing the necessary information, which we have duly acknowledged. But, few of our respondents want to conceal their identity. We respect their position as well.

Contents

1
Understanding Trafficking in Persons

Introduction

Human trafficking has become a serious global issue of unforeseen proportions of the twenty-first century. By its nature of exploitation, human trafficking has also been increasingly referred to as "modern-day slavery"[1], and this has prompted rapid proliferation of international, regional, and national anti-trafficking laws, and inspired states to devote enormous financial and bureaucratic resources to its eradication (Chuang 2014). In fact, it affects every country in the world, irrespective of socio-economic status, history, or political structure and most countries have become a source, a transit, and a destination for victims of this heinous crime either in larger extent or to a lesser degree. It is in true sense becoming an abhorrent crime of today (Clark 2014). The profits from human trafficking are apparently huge and the United Nations Office of Drugs and Crime (UNODC) places human trafficking as the fastest growing and second most profitable form of transnational crime (Amahazion 2015). The trafficking in human beings is one of the greatest criminal phenomena facing the international community today. So far, available literatures on human trafficking are largely focused on sex trafficking or sex work. Human trafficking has become synonymous with trafficking for sex work, which primarily involves women and girls, while trafficking for forced labour, which also involves men and boys, continues to be an overlooked component of global human trafficking (Nicola Piper cited in Presenti 2012).

Trafficking in person is an abhorrent crime of which many of the victims are identified to be originated from developing and transitional nations and this crime has now become a global crime that is considered to be 'modern day slavery' (Gabhan, 2006). It is a growing phenomenon in the world. Over the last decade, the volume of human trafficking has increased though the exact numbers are not known; it is one of the most lucrative criminal trades, next to arms and drug smuggling undertaken by highly organized criminals.[2] The reasons for increasing it, as a global phenomenon, are multiple and complex which also affects rich and poor countries alike. The popular perception of trafficking is the sexual exploitation of women and children; however, children are trafficked for a variety of reasons. There are various social, economic and political conditions, which create a situation of vulnerability specially, for women and children, who were trapped into trafficking. A recent study shows that cultural practice[3], climate changes, environmental issues and poor governance have also become one of the conditions for this vulnerability that leads to this crime.[4] Poverty, increasing trend of migration even within the country, and lack of economic opportunity are some of the major push factors for trafficking in women and children. The problem of commercial sex workers, urbanisation and globalisation, demand for cheap labour, current trend of consumerism are some of the important pull factors for trafficking in human beings. International Communities, under the aegis of the United Nations (UN), made constant effort for preventing and combating in human trafficking by adopting conventions and protocols. Despite various enactments, general penal laws and specific laws for preventing and combating trafficking in human being in India, the North East India emerged to be a hot spot zone of trafficking in women and children and this will be discussed in the subsequent chapters.

Concept of Human Trafficking

The United Nations "Protocol to Prevent, Suppress and Punish Trafficking in Persons, Especially Women and Children, Supplementing the United Nations Convention against Transnational Organized Crime" (otherwise known as the Palermo Protocol) constituted in 2000 has been widely and internationally accepted Convention. According to Article 3 of the UN Protocol, trafficking in persons is defined as:

> ...the recruitment, transportation, transfer, harbouring or receipt of persons, by means of the threat or use of force or other forms of coercion, of abduction, of fraud, of deception, of the abuse of power or of a position of vulnerability or of the giving or receiving of payments or benefits to achieve the consent of a person having control over another person, for the purpose of exploitation (UNODC 2006).

Exploitation here shall include, at a minimum, the exploitation of the prostitution of others or other form of sexual exploitation, forced labour or services, slavery or practices similar to slavery, servitude or the removal of organs (United Nations Office on Drugs and Crime 2014). Thus trafficking can be conceptualised in, first, the transportation of a person; second, force, fraud, or coercion; and, finally, exploitation Rhacel Salazar Parreñas (2012). By this concept, the "consent" of a person, either to be trafficked or smuggled, is irrelevant. (Rhacel 2012) opines that the legal violation under human smuggling pertains to the illicit crossing of nation-state borders, and it is assumed that individuals do this consensually. She further argued that a smuggled person would fall under the broader category of "migrant", as migration generally refers to the voluntary movement of individuals. Yet, like human trafficking, migration does not necessarily involve the crossing of national borders, as smuggling does (Rhacel Salazar Parreñas 2012).

The definition of Palermo Protocol gives more emphasis on coercion as well as exploitation and it thus provides activists as well as states a leeway to prosecute human traffickers and to work against human trafficking in a very wide scope. However, at the same time, Palermo Protocol has been subject to certain critics as "it subsumes almost every kind of illegal migration under trafficking and thus is subject to anti-trafficking laws" (Ann Jordan 2002; Bridget Anderson and Julia O'Connell Davidson 2004 cited Presenti 2012). Further, critics like Doezema (2002) stress that "almost every illegal migrant who engages in sex work could be considered trafficked under this definition" (Presenti 2012) though some of them are engaged in sex work out of "consensual". Thus, the considerable feminist literature on trafficking is centred upon these tricky issues of consent versus coercion in sex work and the fine line between trafficking and migration (Presenti 2012:234).

For Rao and Presenti (2012), if human smuggling is only "largely voluntary" or of "consensual", then the difference between trafficking and illegal migration facilitated by human smugglers is only one of the degrees of abuse. Available literatures show that "even legal migration sometimes involves deception and legal violations on the part of both migrants and those who serve as migration agents" (Presenti 2012). The literature on trafficking in persons suggests that in the case of migration, any abuse and exploitation is expected once the migrant has arrived at the destination, while in the case of human trafficking it began from the origin till the destination. Here, the distinction is that it is tenuous, and, more importantly, it may not always be useful to preserve from a migrant rights perspective.

It has always been a subject to debate both in theory as well as practice. This debate has grown centering on how the problem of trafficking connects to some other relevant issues like prostitution, migration, organized crime, human rights, among other issues (Uddin 2014). Many of the radical feminists consider that prostitution is the main reason behind the crime of human trafficking and it should be abolished (Uddin 2014). On the other hand, liberal feminist/sex worker group, who are in favour of legalizing of prostitution, acknowledges prostitution as sex work and hence argues that migrant sex workers should not fall into the category of trafficked persons, or in other words they claim that sex work is not necessarily the result of trafficking (Samarasinghe cited in Uddin 2014). Whatever the case, human trafficking has been a serious global issue of unforseen proportion. Therefore, apart from the debate over whether trafficking is a problem of prostitution or migration or whether consensual or coerced, we must give more emphasis on the questions like, why does trafficking in person happen in the first place? What are the root causes of trafficking in person? How does trafficking is related to human (in) security? These are some of the questions that need to be taken into account if our purpose is to fight trafficking in person.

Global Overview on Trafficking in Persons

A report from UNODC (2014) reveals that most of the offenders[5] are mostly men, while most of the detected victims are female (mainly women, but also a significant number of juvenile girls). As in a routine way, trafficking, which is a trans-national crime, is often carried out domestically or within a given subregion, and most offenders are convicted in their countries of citizenship. Most of the victims, on the other hand, are often found out to be foreigners in the country where their exploitation was detected. The report also shows that trafficking flows are usually confined to a geographically limited area, either within a country or between neighbouring or relatively close countries. A significant number of foreigners are found to be the offender of trafficking in persons in many of the countries where this crime is common, and many of the victims are also found to be exploited in their own country of citizenship. As reported by UNODC (2014) trans-regional trafficking accounts for nearly a quarter of all trafficking flows albeit it is less common than the domestic or intra-regional types.

Profile of the Offenders

It is important to find out who the offenders are if we have to understand the crime of trafficking in persons. Identifying and analysing the citizenship as well as gender of traffickers can help generate a broader understanding of the profiles of traffickers and their networks, as well as on how they operate. The task of identifying traffickers' citizenship is highly significant, particularly when it comes to cross-border trafficking as there is often a citizenship link between traffickers and victims, as trafficking in persons is a crime that is often operated trans-national. Report from UNODC (2014) reveals that the citizenship of persons convicted for trafficking in persons provided by 64 countries totals up to 5,747 offenders.[6] Information on the gender of suspected, prosecuted and/or convicted offenders was provided by 43, 59 and 64 countries respectively, covering 29,568 persons suspected, 4,915 persons convicted and 10,024 persons prosecuted for trafficking in persons. The data covers the 2010-2012 period (or more recent). The report also reveals that most if not all the citizenship profiles of the people convicted of trafficking in persons show that most offenders are citizens of the country where they were convicted (UNODC 2014). It is found out that more than 6 in 10 are convicted traffickers globally. It is reasonable to expect that the majority of people convicted of nearly any crime would be citizens of the prosecuting country. Even though international mobility is high, most people still live and operate mainly within their own countries.

Although majority of offenders who are convicted are found out to be the citizens of their own country, the UNODC (2014) shows that nearly 35 per cent of convicted traffickers are found out to be foreigners. If fact, this is a larger share of convicted foreigners than what is typically seen for most other crimes, for which foreign citizens generally comprise approximately 10 per cent of those convicted (UNODC 2014). It may be taken by surprise that a greater proportion of women is also convicted of trafficking in persons than of nearly any other crime[7], and the detection of male victims is increasing (United Nations Office on Drugs and Crime 2014). Siegel & Blank (2010) who did a case study in the Netherland also found out that women who are generally perceived to be the victims of trafficking are not always the victims in human trafficking, rather become the perpetrator. It is reported that 38 per cent of suspected offenders are reported to be committed by women during 2010-2012 (UNODC). This is another anomaly in comparison to other types of crime. While the majority, some 62 per cent of suspected traffickers is male, the female share is large. These shares are similar, though somewhat smaller, at other stages of the criminal justice process as well: 32 per cent of prosecuted and 28 per cent of convicted traffickers are women. For most other crimes, the share of females among the total number of convicted persons is in the range of 10-15 per cent. Relatively high female involvement appears to be another characteristic of the crime of trafficking in persons.

Victim Profile

Females, either adult or juvenile are reported to be the majority of the victims detected globally.[8] The overall profile of trafficking victims may be slowly changing, however, as relatively fewer women, but more girls (particularly underage), men and boys are detected globally (UNODC 2014). So far, adult women are detected to be comprised of approximately half the total number of victims of trafficking although it is reported that female victim has declined markedly.[9] During the period of 2010-2012, male victims are also reported to be comprised 25 to 30 per cent among the total number of victims detected globally. The trend of underage boy victims has increased since 2004 (United Nations Office on Drugs and Crime 2014). While increases can be seen for both men and boys, it is more pronounced for men. The key reason seems to be the greater number of detected cases of trafficking for forced labour in many countries, as this type of trafficking involves more male than female victims.

The previously reported trend of an overall lowering of the average age of detected victims has been confirmed by the data collected for the Report of UNODC 2014. Child trafficking, in which victims are below 18 years of age, accounts for more than 30 per cent of the total number of victims detected during the 2010-2012 period. The proportion of detected child victims has increased significantly in recent years. However, increasing shares of children among the detected victims were not witnessed across all regions or areas. While Africa and the Middle East, North and Central America, as well as some countries in South America did register clear increases during the period of 2010-2012, in other regions of the world, such as Europe and Central Asia as well as South Asia, East Asia and the Pacific, child trafficking remained relatively stable compared to the period of 2007-2010.

The patterns of trafficking in persons continue to show pronounced regional differences. Children comprise the majority of victims detected in Africa and the Middle East, accounting for more than 60 per cent of the victims in this region. In Europe and Central Asia, trafficking in persons mainly concerns adult victims, as they comprise 83 per cent of the victims detected there. South Asia, East Asia and the Pacific and the Americas report similar age profile breakdowns, with adults comprising about two thirds of the detected victims, with children making up the remaining one third.

Responses to Trafficking in Persons

It may be mentioned here that modern day trafficking in person is not a recent phenomenon although there is growing concern about this issue in recent times. Its origin can be dated back to the late nineteenth century where it starts with the movement against the Trans-Atlantic slave trade (particularly the white women for prostitution) which is popularly known as movement against the abolition of "white slave trade". With the movement against the white slave trade, the International Agreement for the Suppression of White Slave Traffic was formed during 1904-1910. This international legal instrument was the first of its kind constituted to abolish human trafficking in trafficking in persons history. Thereafter, a series of legal instruments (with or without amendments of the above mentioned instrument) came into being for the criminalisation of human traffickers. Some of them are, Trafficking in Women and Children (1921), International Convention for the Suppression of the Traffic in Women of Full Age (1933), Suppression of the Traffic in Persons and of the Exploitation of the Prostitution of Others (1949), etc. These series of instruments mentioned above were either inadequate as a law to be applied or enforced and the concept is often confused with human smuggling and migration, given that these practices also involve the movement of persons albeit there are important differences between them (Rhacel Salazar Parreñas 2012). As a result, these early anti-trafficking conventions above mentioned were eventually consolidated into the 1949 Convention known as the Suppression of the Traffic in Persons and of the Exploitation of the Prostitution of Others, which basically referred to trafficking as a problem associated with prostitution (Uddin 2014). Thus, having started in early decades, a series of international instruments against trafficking were adopted throughout the twentieth century.

The United Nations adopted the Universal Declaration on Human Rights, 1948 to set an international standard and norms for promotion and protection of human rights in the world. Further, it adopted the Convention on the Elimination of all Form of Discrimination against Women, in 1979 with an objective to improve the situation of women in the World. Article 6 of the Convention obligates the states parties to take all appropriate measures including enactment of legislation to suppress all forms of traffic in women and exploitation of prostitution of women. The World Conference on Human Rights, held in Vienna in 1993, also stresses the importance of working towards the elimination of all forms of sexual harassment, exploitation and trafficking in women. India has also signed the said convention on the 30th July, 1980 and ratified on the 9th July, 1993.

In relation to children, the Convention on the Rights of Child, 1989 was adopted and opened for ratification to the member states. Article 35 of the Convention stipulates that states parties shall take all appropriate national, bilateral and multilateral measures to prevent the abduction of, the sale of or traffic in children for any purpose or in any form. The Convention has been supplemented by two other Optional Protocols adopted in 2000. The second Optional Protocol to the Convention on the Rights of the Child, on the Sale of Children, Child Prostitution and Child Pornography obligates the states parties to prohibit such acts by making it an offence punishable under law. Article 9 (2) of the Optional Protocol states that states parties shall take all feasible measures with the aims of ensuring all appropriate assistance to victims of such offence including their full social re-integration and their full physical and psychological recovery. The Protocol also spells out the need for promoting and strengthening international co-operation in order to address the root cause such as, poverty and underdevelopment, contributing to the vulnerability of children to the sale of children, child prostitution, child pornography and child sex tourism. India is one of the parties to Child Right Convention, 1989 as well to the First Optional Protocol on Involvement of Children in Armed Conflict 2000 and the Second Optional Protocol on the Sale of Children, Child Prostitution and Child Pornography, 2000. She has to fulfil the international obligation by implementing the provisions of the CRC, 1989 and its optional protocols under international law and practice.

The United Nations Convention against Trans-Organised Crime, adopted by the General Assembly in 2000, is the main international instrument in the fight against trans-organised crime. It has been supplemented by three Optional Protocols including the Protocol to Prevent, Suppress and Punish Trafficking in person, specially Women and Children, 2000. Two important purposes of the protocol are: (i) To prevent and combat trafficking in persons, paying particular attention to women and children; and (ii) To protect and assist the victims of such trafficking with full respect for their human rights. Article 3 of the Protocol defines trafficking in persons as the recruitment, transportation, transfer, harbouring or receipt of persons by means of the threat or use of force or other form of coercion, of abduction, of fraud, of deception, of the abuse of power or of a position of vulnerability or of saving or receiving of payments or benefits to achieve the consent of a person having control over another person for the purpose of exploitation of prostitution of other or other forms of sexual exploitation. It further states that exploitation shall include at a minimum, the exploitation, the prostitution of others or other forms of sexual exploitation, force labour or services, slavery or practices similar to slavery, servitude or the removal of organs. The Convention also urges the states parties to establish comprehensive policies, programmes and other measures to prevent and combat trafficking in persons and to protect victims of trafficking in persons, especially women and children from re-victimization. It is also the duty of the states parties to protect the privacy and identity of victims of trafficking by making legal proceeding relating to such trafficking confidential.

The United Nations has created its own monitoring and investigating mechanism for promotion and protection of human rights. Human Rights Council appoints special rapporteurs with the mandate to investigate, monitor and recommend solution to human rights problems. The Special Rapporteur on trafficking in person specially women and children has been working since 2004 under the mandate of the Council to investigate, monitor, assess and verify complaints of alleged cases of trafficking in women and children. The UN Special Rapporteur on Human Trafficking, Special Rapporteur on Sale on Children pornography, Special Rapporteur on Contemporary forms of Slavery, and the Special Rappoteurs on the Human Rights of Migrants Workers received the information that an estimated no. of 70,000 bonded children labour from Nepal and Bangladesh worked at the so-called rat mines of Jaintia Hill of Meghalaya located in the north-eastern state of India. The Special Rapporteurs sought clarification of that fact from the Government of India and requested information on investigation, carried out in relation to individuals who were implicated in trafficking or selling the children to the rat mines and keeping them in bonded labour. The Special Rapporteur also sought information on policies and preventive measures, undertaken to combat human trafficking, sale of children and sexual exploitation of the children in India. The Special Rapporteur regretted that government had not provided a reply to the communication and urged the government to take up appropriate measure to protect the rights of children concerned immediately.

At the regional level, the SAARC Convention on Preventing and Combating Trafficking in Women and Children was unanimously adopted by the SAARC countries on January 5, 2002 in Kathmandu. The purpose of this Convention is to promote cooperation amongst Member States so that they may effectively deal with the various aspects of prevention, interdiction and suppression of trafficking in women and children; the repatriation and rehabilitation of victims of trafficking and prevent the use of women and children in international prostitution networks, particularly where the countries of the SAARC region are the countries of origin, transit and destination. Article 1 (3) of the Convention defines trafficking as the moving, selling or buying of women and children for prostitution within and outside a country for monetary or other considerations with or without the consent of the person subjected to trafficking. Apart from having incorporated provisions for extending legal assistance among the SAARC Countries in respect of investigations, inquiries, trials or other proceedings in the requesting State in respect of offences under this Convention, article VIII of the Convention makes those offences referred in the Convention as extraditable offences under Extradition Treaty.

State of Global Response to Trafficking in Persons

The Protocol to Prevent, Suppress and Punish Trafficking in Persons, Especially Women and Children, which supplements the United Nations Convention against Trans-national Organized Crime, came into force in December 2003. The impact of the Protocol on the national legislative responses around the world has been reported to be very strong. UNODC (2014) reported that by the end of the year 2006, three years after the Protocol entered into force, only 28 per cent of countries did not have specific offence that criminalized trafficking in persons, or even just some forms of this crime. It was reported that almost two thirds of countries did not have this in 2003 when this Protocol was established. By 2014, UNODC reported that the countries that do not have specific legislation that criminalizes trafficking in persons have reduced to five per cent. Eighty-five per cent, i.e. 146 countries out of 173 countries that was considered for analysis, has succeeded in criminalising all aspects of trafficking in persons explicitly listed in the UN Trafficking in Persons Protocol (United Nations Office on Drugs and Crime 2014).

UNODC (2014) report reveals that nearly ten per cent of the covered countries, i.e. around seventeen to eighteen counties out of 173 countries that were taken for analysis, have partial legislation so far. Of course, these countries may criminalize trafficking in persons specifically, but their legislation may only cover some victims (particularly, only children, women and/or foreigners) or certain forms of exploitation (for instances sexual exploitation) among other issues. UNODC (2014) also reported that nearly five per cent, i.e. nearly nine countries out of 173 countries that were taken for analysis, do not have any offence in their legislation that specifically criminalises trafficking in persons, or even just some forms of it. It is likely that instances of trafficking may be prosecuted in these countries by leveraging other articles of the criminal code, such as slavery, forced labour, pimping, child stealing or others (which may also happen in countries that have specific legislation on trafficking in persons) (United Nations Office on Drugs and Crime 2014). However, it is very unlikely that these instruments are tailored to address the issue of victim assistance. Moreover, the sanctions for the traffickers may not be commensurate to the gravity of the crimes committed.

In terms of regional study, Africa and Middle East region found out to be the part of the world that requires strenuous effort to fill the legislative gap more than other countries' needs when analysing the details in terms of legislative coverage. Around eight countries in this region appear to be lagging behind to criminalise trafficking in persons offences. Further, within this region, ten countries fall into those countries with offences that criminalize only some aspects of trafficking (United Nations Office on Drugs and Crime 2014). On the other hand, it is also very important to consider the population size of countries without adequate legislation in place. When this is taken into consideration, regions other than Africa also emerge as problematic.

Regions like Asia and South America Large, which are among the most densely populated countries still have partial legislation. As a result, in these countries, there are persons living in trafficking situations constituting an offence according to the international standards, but who may not be considered as trafficking victims by the national authorities as these are using legal definitions not in line with the UN Trafficking in Persons Protocol (United Nations Office on Drugs and Crime 2014).

It is reported that around two billion people, i.e., about one third of the world's population, live in a situation where trafficking is not criminalized as required by the UN Trafficking in Persons Protocol. This may be happened due to lack of specific legislative instruments or due to partiality in criminalizing the offence. This situation combined with a very low number of convictions makes trafficking in persons a crime of vast impunity. UNODC (2014) has also pointed out that large chunk of the world's population is without the protection and support enforced by the UN Trafficking in Persons Protocol, as the legislation of their respective countries does not comply with the UN Protocol. This leaves the victims of human trafficking with no right to obtain from the said Protocol. In such a situation, there became a risk that the traffickers who are exploiting these victims may face light punishment or no criminal charges even when law enforcement authorities detect them (offenders). In addition to the above, cooperation with national authorities of other countries is often very difficult to get, as country level legislation may be incompatible.

The data on investigations, prosecutions and convictions collected for the period 2010-2012 for the preparation of 2014 UNODC report show that the number of convictions for the crime of trafficking in persons remains very low. Nearly fifteen per cent, i.e. around 19 of the 128 countries covered by the data collection did not record a single conviction. Another large share of the countries covered, about one fourth, recorded a limited number of convictions, between 1 and 10, in at least one of the years between 2010 and 2012. About 40 per cent of the countries covered reported more than 10 convictions, out of which, some 16 per cent had more than 50 convictions in at least one of the years considered here. The number of convictions and their distribution around the world remained stable or hardly changed positively.

The lack of specific legislative instruments or partiality in criminalizing the offence may be largely related to the data of conviction for offense in trafficking in persons. In addition to this, limitations of comprehensive as well as reliable data also act as a major hurdle that prevents a comprehensive comparison between the number of convictions and the number of detected victims.[10] Among the countries that reported on both indicators, most of the countries with few or no convictions also identified or assisted a very limited number of victims. About one third of the countries with few or no recorded convictions, however, detected a significant number of victims. While this suggests that local institutions are responding to the trafficking occurring in their countries by identifying and possibly assisting victims, this does raise the question of why this response does not turn into a final sentence for the traffickers. It is reported that for some of the countries that record few convictions and a significant number of victims, the use of other offences to convict the traffickers could explain why there is no correlation between the detection of victims and a proper criminal justice response. In other cases, it appears that the identification of a victim does not lead to the prosecution of a trafficker. This situation leads to the victimisation of the victims of trafficking in persons. Thus, lacking confidence upon the national authorities, many offences are not reported by many of the victims.

In an overall global scenario, the criminal justice response shows hardly any change in recent years. In an assessment of how many countries reported increases or decreases in the absolute number of convictions per year during the period 2010-2012, for the compilation of UNODC-2014, confirms this. It shows that vast majority of the countries reported a relatively stable number of convictions over the period 2010-2012, while just 13 per cent saw a noticeable increase. On the other hand, another 10 per cent of countries recorded decreasing trends over the same period. This shows that from a global, aggregated perspective, the situation remained stable. Moreover, the share of countries reporting stable conviction trends has not changed significantly since 2003. It is reported that between 2003 and 2007, the share of countries with stable or unclear trends was 71 per cent, between 2007 and 2010, it was 60 per cent but between 2010 and 2012, the share was 77 per cent. Similarly, the share of countries with increasing number of convictions decreased from 21 to 13 per cent.

The above mentioned data shows that the number of countries that successfully manage to punish at least some of the traffickers that operate in their territories is very limited. It also shows that the situation has not changed in the short to medium term. As more countries introduced adequate legislation over the last ten years, a gradual increase of convictions worldwide was expected in those countries where trafficking in persons was known to be a problem. Moreover, over the last few years, there has been a perception that proper criminal justice responses would lead to a rising number of convictions some years after the entry of the UN Trafficking in Persons Protocol into force. This has not happened, or perhaps only to a very limited extent. While more countries in the world now have solid legislation, the number of convictions is still stable at a very low level more or less everywhere. The wide regional differences make different levels of the overall criminal justice response at the national level and at different stages of the criminal justice process.

Regional Overview on Trafficking in Persons

Regions like Europe and Central Asia, America, Africa and Middle East, South Asia, East Asia and Pacific region are covered in most of the studies for trafficking in persons. Profiles of the victims as well as offender and the response to the offences committed are apparently different from one region to other region. For that matter, it is required to analyse those issues separately. UN dataset and UN reports on trafficking in persons are mainly referred, as other reliable as well as comprehensive data are missing. The region of Europe and Central Asia is divided into two sub-regions, namely Western and Central Europe, as well as Eastern Europe and Central Asia. The two sub-regions display some similarities in terms of the patterns and flows of trafficking in persons. Other aspects are quite different, particularly in relation to trafficking flows. Since the data from this region is solid, particularly for Western and Central Europe, the two sub-regions will be presented in separate sections.

(a) Issue of Trafficking in Persons in Europe and Central Asia

Western and Central Europe is a region that is reported to be a significant place of origin as well as important destination for trafficking in persons. Countries in Central Europe and the Balkans are mainly origin areas for cross-border trafficking into the rest of

Europe. Significant levels of domestic trafficking are also detected in these countries. The richer countries in Western and Southern Europe are generally considered to be the destinations for victims who are trafficked from other regions (particularly from Asia, Africa and the Americas) and for European victims trafficked from Central Europe and the Balkans (United Nations Office on Drugs and Crime 2014). Most of these countries also report considerable levels of domestic trafficking. On the other hand, one of the key characteristics of trafficking in persons in Eastern Europe and Central Asia is the strong involvement of women, both as traffickers and victims.

Profile of the Offenders

Western and Central European countries convict citizens of their own country and foreigners in near equal proportions. More than half of the offenders convicted during the period, 2010-2012 were citizens of the country of conviction. About 30 per cent of the traffickers were foreigners from countries within the same sub-region. Compared to the global average, countries in Western and Central Europe convict fewer own citizens (even though they do make up a majority of offenders) but more foreigners from within the sub-region. Considering origins from outside Western and Central Europe, the largest share is made up of traffickers from Africa and the Middle East. This group accounts for some 10 per cent of the total number of people convicted. Most of these offenders are citizens of countries in West and North Africa. However, the relevance of West African traffickers (some 6 per cent of the convicted offenders) is limited in comparison to the large share of victims from this region that are detected in Western and Central Europe.

Other significant groups of foreign traffickers from outside the sub-region are Asians and citizens of countries in the Americas. These groups account for some five per cent of the offenders in this region. Offenders from Eastern Europe and Central Asia comprise a small, but significant share, with two per cent of the total. The citizenship profiles of the foreign offenders broadly mirror the profiles of the detected foreign trafficking victims, at least by major regional aggregations. Fewer women are convicted in this sub-region that is somewhat lower than the global average.

It is reported that around twenty three per cent of those prosecuted and/or convicted of trafficking in persons in this sub-region are women, compared to some 28 per cent at the global level (UNODC 2014).

The report further shows that the countries within this sub-region reported significant differences in the shares of women who are prosecuted and convicted. Some countries in the Balkans have very low shares of convictions of women. In other countries, including in the Baltic area, women comprise nearly one third of the convicted trafficking offenders. However, in terms of *Eastern Europe and Central Asia* almost half of the traffickers are found to be women. Women are detected to be involved in trafficking in persons than most other crimes, a female offending rate of some 50 per cent is exceptional as the global average for trafficking in persons is around 30 per cent.

The vast majority of the traffickers convicted in this sub-region, i.e. more than 90 per cent, are local citizens convicted in their own countries. About 8 per cent are foreigners from countries within Eastern Europe and Central Asia.

Profile of the Victims

On an average, it is found that more adult victims that comprised mostly women victims are detected in Western and Central Europe as compared to other sub-regions. A majority of the detected victims of trafficking in persons in Western and Central Europe, i.e. some 63 per cent, are adult women, whereas the second largest group is found to be adult men, who account for 19 per cent of the total number of victims. Data from the UN reveals that adult victims thus comprise more than 80 per cent of all the detected victims in this sub-region. The issue of child trafficking in this sub-region is apparently not as common as in other regions. Report reveals that children account for just 20 per cent of the detected victims, whereas globally, this group makes up nearly one third of the victims. Comparatively, girls are apparently more than boys when victim of trafficking is concerned in this sub-region. The data of UNODC reveals that out of every five children trafficked in this sub-region, four are girls and one is a boy. Although significant detection of women victims in the entire region has already been mentioned, *Eastern Europe and Central Asia* account for 77 per cent, which is reported to be particularly high turning out to be the highest share of women victims of any sub-region.

In this sub-region, about 15 per cent of the detected victims are men. UNODC 2014 report shows that the adult victims accounting to be well above 90 per cent in this sub-region, appear to be of large share in a global perspective. Child trafficking or child victims appear to be comparatively low in Eastern Europe and Central Asia as compared to adult victims. The report shows that only about 8 per cent of the detected victims are children. Child trafficking in this sub-region is mainly concerns with girls that is also the similar case of Western and Central Europe.

Response to Trafficking

All the countries in this sub-region have national legislation that is in line with the UN Trafficking in Persons Protocol when we discuss about legislation. The historical evolution of the legislation in this part of the world was, to a considerable extent, affected by the entry into force of the Protocol in December 2003. More than half of the countries amended their criminal code after this date to introduce a specific offence on trafficking in persons that was in line with the international standards. While several of the countries had specific legislation before December 2003, the offences were often introduced either in the year 2002 or earlier in 2003. So for many of these countries as well, the legislation was amended as a result of the political push generated by the Trafficking in Persons Protocol that was adopted by the Member States in the year 2000.

A further geographical analysis of the report shows that the countries in Central Europe and the Balkans were the quickest in setting up their legislative counter-trafficking framework. Among the 18 countries with proper legislation in place in 2003, 6 were in Western Europe, while 12 were in Central Europe and the Balkans. The gap was quickly closed, however, as after just five years; most of the countries had adopted proper legislation to combat trafficking in persons. In Western and Central Europe, eight countries recorded more than 50 convictions in at least one year during the 2010-2012 period. On an average, 30 per cent of trafficking in persons in Western and Central Europe received a conviction in the first instance. About half of those prosecuted got a first instance conviction.

Similar to Western and Central Europe, all countries in *Eastern Europe and Central Asia* have legislation in line with the UN Trafficking in Persons Protocol today. Like the Western and Central Europe, all the countries in this sub-region have introduced legislation in the year that complies with the said Protocol. It is reported that the number of persons convicted per 1,00,000 population in Europe and Central Asia is higher in comparison to the rest of the world, and the average rates in Eastern Europe are somewhat higher than in Western Europe. However, the highest rates of convictions per population in Europe, and in the world, are registered in the Balkans, with a peak of 2 convictions per 1,00,000 populations (United Nations Office on Drugs and Crime 2014).

(b) Issue of Trafficking in Persons in Americas

Americas here is described as the region that consists of the sub-regions such as, North and Central America, the Caribbean, and South America. These sub-regions display many similar traits in terms of the profile of the traffickers as well as the profile of the victims albeit it shows a different picture in terms of flow i.e. destination or origin of the trafficking in persons.

Profile of the Offenders

As in other parts of the world, most of the offenders in the Americas are people convicted of trafficking in persons in their own country of citizenship that account for about 80 per cent of the total number of convicted offenders. Report reveals that about 17 per cent of the offenders are citizens of other countries, whereas about three per cent are traffickers from countries in other regions. Some of the traffickers in this group are citizens of typical destination countries for South American victims. The report reveals that most foreign traffickers are convicted in destination countries. It also reveals that the participation of foreign traffickers in countries of origin in this region seems to be higher than in most other parts of the world. As it happens in other parts of the regions, similar case occurs in America too, in terms of female offenders. Female traffickers in this region appear to be relatively high accounting to about 40 per cent of the total prosecutions as well as convictions. These shares are similar in both sub-regions, even if somewhat higher in South America. A closer look reveals that Central American countries record higher shares of female involvement in the trafficking process while Canada records the lowest.

Profile of the Victims

So far adult victims make up 70 per cent of the trafficking victims while child victims make up the remaining 30 per cent. Some differences are found out in terms of the profiles of detected victims between the sub-regions of America. It is found out that in North America and in the Southern Cone of South America, adult trafficking accounts for a larger share of victims than the regional average. While in the Central America and in the northern part of South America child trafficking is found to be relatively high. The report of UNODC 2014 shows that most of the detected child victims are girls. It says that out of every three children detected as victims, two are girls and one is a boy. This applies to the whole of the American region. Adult female victims are still higher as compared to the adults male victims in this region. Adult women account for about half of all the detected victims in this region.

Response to Trafficking in Persons

As far as the legislation in this region is concerned, it complies with the UN Protocol, most of the countries have specific legislation today. All North and Central American countries have a specific offence in line with the UN Trafficking in Persons Protocol. Among those considered, one country in the Caribbean lacks a specific offence on trafficking in persons, while four countries in South America and the Caribbean criminalize only some aspects of trafficking in persons. Most of the countries in this part of the world did not include trafficking in persons in their criminal code before the entry into force of the Trafficking in Persons Protocol in 2003. In fact, only three countries had a specific offence in line with international standards at that time, while five had partial legislation. A few years later, the situation improved. In 2008, almost half of the countries in the Western Hemisphere had legislation on trafficking in persons in compliance with the international standards. Nowadays, the situation has further improved as a vast majority of the countries have full-fledged legislation. The criminal justice response in the Western Hemisphere shows that among the countries considered, only the United States of America and Peru reported more than 50 convictions for trafficking in persons per year. Some countries in Central America and in the Caribbean did not report a single conviction, while the rest of the countries registered below or around 10 convictions per year.

(c) Issue of Trafficking in Persons in Asia and Pacific

Asia and Pacific region is reported to be the main origin for trafficking in persons. For South Asia, human trafficking discourses have been mostly dominated by two approaches: prostitution/sex work approach and migration approach. Illegal migration or prostitution still dominates the discourse of trafficking in these countries, which prioritizes state security over human security and does not adequately address the root causes of trafficking and the insecurity of trafficked individuals. According to the United Nations Office on Drug and Crime (UNODC)[11], 1,50,000 people are trafficked within South Asia annually making the region second only to South East Asia in terms of the prevalence of human trafficking. In fact, UNODC ranks Bangladesh, India, Nepal and Pakistan as countries of high origin. Further, India and Pakistan are also ranked as high destination countries. It is particularly considered that India has become the world's largest labour trafficking country with hundreds of thousands of sex trafficking victims. Moreover, this includes millions of bonded labourers including forced child labourers. As such, India happens to be one of the sources, destinations and transits countries for human trafficking specially issues relating to commercial sexual exploitation and forced labour.

Profile of the Offenders

As per the report, 97 per cent of the offenders convicted fall under the local citizen of this region (UNODC 2014). It is also reported that about 3 per cent of the offenders convicted in this region are foreigners, and almost all of them come from the same sub-region.

This can be explained by the fact that most of the trafficking bound for this region originate from the same area. Although Europe and Central Asia, North Africa and the Middle East, or the Americas are the significant destinations for the Asian victims, very few people from these regions are detected as offenders. This suggests that trafficking flows are either manoeuvred in the origin countries, or trafficking networks operating in the destination countries recruit local traffickers to 'collect' victims from their origins.

Regarding the gender profiles of offenders, it seems that women and men are prosecuted in relatively equal proportions, depending somewhat on the country concerned. Limited data on the profile of the persons convicted does not permit a comprehensive analysis on the gender distribution of the offenders. Due to lack of comprehensive information on the gender profile of offenders, there is hardly any information from prosecutions or convictions, although information on women involvement in trafficking in person is an open secret. It is reported that more than 40 per cent of the persons investigated for trafficking in persons in India were females.

Profile of the Victims

It is reported that vast majority of the victims detected in Asia are females, either adults or underage girls (UNODC 2014). Male victims are also found in this region although it appears to be comparatively low against the global average. Report shows that it accounts for about 17 per cent of the total number of victims detected. Child victims are apparently high in this region. In terms of child trafficking, South Asia becomes second only to the share data recorded in Sub-Saharan Africa (UNODC 2014). It is reported that Bangladesh recorded a high level of child trafficking, while in Nepal, women remain the most frequently reported victims of trafficking. However, lack of information and reliable data is the setback in giving a comprehensive picture of child trafficking.

Response to Trafficking in Persons

It has found out that most of the countries in this region have legislation that criminalizes all aspects listed in the Trafficking in Persons Protocol. Only a few countries still have partial legislation.

Large populations in these countries are an element of concern, as discussed in the global overview. Before December 2003, just four countries had a specific offence on trafficking in persons in line with international standard. Half of the countries did not criminalize this crime as such, and 40 per cent had partial legislation that mainly focused on trafficking of women or trafficking for sexual exploitation. Thus, trafficking for forced labour or trafficking in men was not yet considered as crimes in several countries. So far, some countries from South East Asia as well as from Pacific has come up with some comprehensive legislation while many of the South Asian and East Asian countries still lack proper legislation that complies with the international standard. No doubt, the number of convictions in this part of the world is reported to be higher than other regions, but certain factors should be taken into consideration while considering this matter, such as, large populations, partial legislation and the unavailability of reliable data.

Conclusion

Judging by news headlines, human trafficking is a recent phenomenon. In fact, the coerced movement of people across borders is as old as the laws of supply and demand. What is new is the volume of the traffic and the realization that we have done little to stem the tide. We must look beyond our raw emotions if we are ever to stop those who trade in human lives.

Notes

1. Síle Nic Gabhan, "Human Trafficking: A Twenty-First Century Slavery", *The Furrow* 57, no. 10 (2006): 528-537.
2. Khan, I. (n.d.). *Child Trafficking in India: A Concern.* Retrieved November 17, 2016
3. 'Devadasi' system (temple dancer, particularly girls from lower caste group) is an old system, rather an old cultural and traditional practice that largely contributes to sexual related crimes including child trafficking in India. For details, see Kumar, A. (2015). *Status of Child Trafficking and Laws related to it.* National Law University and Judicial Academy, Assam. Guwahati: NCPCR. Also see, Najar, J.L. *Human Trafficking in India.*

4. Kamier, T.L. (2015). *Indigenous Women and Human Trafficking in the Mekong Region: Policy Overview and Community Response.* Chiang Mai: Asia Indigenous Peoples Pact (AIPP).
5. In the United Nations Global Plan of Action to Combat Trafficking in Persons, Member States requested for the present report to focus on the patterns and flows of trafficking in persons. 'Patterns' refer to the profiles of traffickers and victims; that is, their citizenship, age and gender as well as the forms of exploitation. 'Flows' refer to the geographic dimension of trafficking, with a 'flow' defined as one origin country and one destination country with at least five detected victims during 2010-2012 reporting period. For details see United Nations Office on Drugs and Crime, *Global Report on Trafficking in Persons 2014,* Annual Report (New York: United Nations, 2014).
6. United Nations Office on Drugs and Crime, *Global Report on Trafficking in Persons 2014,* Annual Report (New York: United Nations, 2014).
7. See Dina Siegel & Sylvia de Blank, "Women who traffic women: the role of women in human trafficking networks – Dutch cases", *Global Crime* (Routledge) 11, no. 4 (November 2010): 436-447.
8. An analysis of the profiles of detected trafficking victims over the period 2010-2012. See United Nations Office on Drugs and Crime, *Global Report on Trafficking in Persons 2014,* Annual Report (New York: United Nations, 2014).
9. Around 80 countries provided the information on the age and gender of trafficking victims. A total of 31,766 victims were detected between 2010 and 2012 whose age and gender were reported. For details, see United Nations Office on Drugs and Crime, *Global Report on Trafficking in Persons 2014,* Annual Report (New York: United Nations, 2014).
10. Smriti Rao & Christina Presenti, "Understanding Human Trafficking Origin: A Cross-Country Empirical Analysis", *Feminist Economics* 18, no. 2 (2012): 231-263.
11. United Nations Office on Drugs and Crime. (2014). *Global Report on Trafficking in Persons 2014.* New York: United Nations.

2

Child Trafficking and North-East India

Introduction

India has been a source, destination and transit country for human trafficking. The Union Home Minister Shri Rajnath Singh, while inaugurating the National Conference on Anti-Human Trafficking 2015, has stated that Human Trafficking is a very sensitive and serious issue and termed it as a borderless organised crime. He cited that more than 1.5 lakh people (as per UN Office on Drugs and Crime) were reported as victims in a single year in South Asia.[1] It is reported that India is the main recipient of an estimated 1,50,000 women and girls trafficked into India from South Asia to feed the commercial sex industry. In addition, India is also reported to be the source and transit country for the sex trafficking of women and children from and to the Middle East. On the other hand, more than two million women and children are trapped in commercial sex work in the red-light districts of India. The Indian government estimates that the vast majority of the 5,00,000 children in the sex industry are girls. A little over 50 per cent of the total commercial sex workers in India are from Nepal and Bangladesh (Shamim cited in Sarkar 2014). The prevalence of girl sex workers from Nepal and Bangladesh can be attributed to prevailing abject poverty and ignorance in both these countries compared with India. However, because of the nature of this crime, it is hard to track, therefore making it impossible to have exact figures regarding the crime.[2] However, some reports reveal that 90 per cent of trafficking occurs domestically (intra-state or inter-state), and 10 per cent occurs across national borders. The country serves as a destination for persons trafficked from neighbouring countries such as Nepal and Bangladesh, and as a transit country for individuals being trafficked to the Middle East and other parts of the world. In addition to this, India is a source country for individuals trafficked to Europe, the Middle East and North America.[3]

According to India's National Crime Records Bureau, a total of 5,466 incidents of crime under various provisions of laws relating to human trafficking were reported in the country during the year 2014 and 3,940 in the year 2013. The crimes relating to human trafficking have increased from 0.3 per cent in 2013 to 0.4 per cent during the year 2014. The incidents of human trafficking have got a rising trend during the period from 2009 to 2014. The crime under human trafficking during the year 2014 has increased by 59.7 per cent over 2010. There has been an increasing trend of children being trafficked from the states of Jharkhand, Chhattisgarh, Odisha, Assam, Manipur, West Bengal and Madhya Pradesh for the purpose of domestic labour. The trafficking of children is being undertaken by illegal placement agencies. Many of these placement agencies are operating from Delhi and the National Capital Region. These placement agencies are earning huge profits by bringing in children from these states (UNODC, cited in Sarkar 2014).

It is a matter of contentment that after a long delay India has finally ratified the UN protocol on human trafficking on 5 May 2011, along with conventions against internationally organised crime and corruption. In fact, ratification of this convention means that it is now binding on India to develop a law that conforms to the international convention and its provisions. Nevertheless, traffickers of forced labour now come within the purview of the law in the country. Thus, the criminal gangs involved in large-scale kidnappings, abductions and forced labour of children go scot-free as the laws in the country are more biased towards prosecuting the employers or pimps in the case of prostitution. The concern is that India lacked a comprehensive definition of human trafficking to provide a common platform for the different Indian states to use in legislation and enforcement (Sarkar 2014). On the other hand, trafficking has not been regarded as an organised crime in India. Thus provisions relevant to such crime are not utilised in enforcement. Also, legislation and enforcement have often failed to distinguish between the traffickers and the victims, so survivors are often punished rather than perpetrators.

As such, a massive decline of the (trafficking) crime shown at official reports can be seriously contentious because it is very difficult to judge or estimate the scale of the phenomenon; and collecting reliable information is one of the toughest exercises due to the clandestine nature of the operation.

Table: International Conventions Related to Human Trafficking[4]

Sl. No.	*Name of the Convention*	*Status for India*
1.	UN Convention on the Rights of the Child	Ratified on 11 December, 1992
2.	Optional Protocol to CRC on Safe of Children, Child Prostitutions, Child Pornography	Signed on 15 November, 2004
3.	Optional Protocol to CRC on Involvement of Children in Armed Conflict	Signed on 15 November, 2004
4.	Protocol to Prevent, Suppress and Punish Trafficking in Persons Especially Women and Children	Ratified on 5 May, 2011
5.	Convention on the Elimination of All Forms of Discrimination Against Women (CEDAW)	Ratified on 9 July, 1993
6.	SAARC Convention on Prevention and Combating Trafficking in Women and Children for Prostitution (2002) and SAARC Convention on Regional Arrangements for Promotion of Child Welfare in South Asia	Signed on 5 January, 2002
7.	Covenant on Economic, Social and Cultural Rights	Ratified on 10 July 1979
8.	Covenant on Civil and Political Rights	Ratified on 10 July 1979
9.	Convention on Elimination of Racial Discrimination	Ratified on 4 January, 1969
10.	Convention Against Torture	Signed on 4 October, 1997
11.	ILO Convention No. 105: Abolition of Forced Labour, 1957	Ratified on 18 May, 2000

Human Trafficking in North-east India

The National Commission for Protection of Child Rights (NCPCR) reported that the states of Manipur, Assam, Meghalaya, Nagaland and Arunachal Pradesh were the 'source' states in the North East from where children as young as five year old were trafficked in the name of free education. Trafficking in Person Report 2010, published by the United States, department of states carried the evidence of NGO report on duping of girls from North East India with promise to providing job and then forcing them into prostitution as well as forced marriage. It is also reported that brides are also in high demand in the state of Haryana and other Northern states of India due to the low sex ratio caused by sex selective abortion. Assam stands top among the North Eastern States registering a total of 149 cases of human trafficking while, Manipur is second with 22 cases of human trafficking. Mizoram, Sikkim and Tripura have not reported a single incident of human trafficking according to the National Crime Record Bureau Report 2013. But the report is being questioned by many as it fails to reflect the ground reality. For instance, trafficking cases of Assam have jumped from 407 recorded in 2014 to 1,494 cases in 2015. It also links to the increasing demand in the cities for all forms and purposes of trafficking. Major cities like Delhi, Mumbai, Bangalore and Chennai are both consuming areas as well as transit grounds, as children are sent to Arab countries through these cities. Delhi and Mumbai, of course, are the main transit grounds for International trafficking. Tripura has emerged as a safe passage for those who are involved in child trafficking business from Bangladesh to West Asia, especially Dubai.

Many cases of child trafficking are recently begun to report in local dailies of the North Eastern States of India. It is reported in one of the local dailies in Imphal that altogether 76 children hailing from Manipur and Assam were rescued by the Child Welfare Committee in the state of Tamil Nadu. These children were trafficked/kept at an unrecognized children home in Magappair, Tamil Nadu. The National Commission for Protection of Child Rights acknowledged the case and recommended to provide proper residential educational rehabilitation of children from vulnerable families in the source area and to introduce effective monitoring mechanism at the block, sub-district, state and central level. It has also been reported in 'the Hindu' (newspaper) that the Guwahati Child Line discovered that all the 24 trafficked minor boys were from the North Cachar Hills District of Assam. Goa police rescued 11 girls, out of which 6 girls were from Nagaland while the rest were from Mizoram from a beauty parlour in Oct. 2010. The girls who were above 18 years of age, alleged that the owner tried to force them into the flesh trade.

The state of Meghalaya, albeit not as grave as in the state of

Assam or Manipur, began to be affected by this heinous trafficking crime.[5] In the state of Nagaland, it has been reported that 29 (twenty nine) children who are from Peren district were rescued from a Home in Andhra Pradesh in the year 2009. These children had been through various physical, social, emotional and mental traumas, and were rescued and repatriated to Nagaland. In another case, in 2011, 6 Naga children from Peren district were also rescued from Hope Home, Kolkata, West Bengal. Of these children, one girl child was only 2 years old. Her mother had given her up, as she could not afford to look after her. SCPS Nagaland coordinated with Childline Kolkata to rescue those children. The officials of SCPS and the State Juvenile Police units went and rescued the children and repatriated them back to their families. The DCPO, Peren along with the counsellors and legal officers are in constant touch with these families and children. Smt. Imti also informed that the SCPS is in process of providing sponsorships and foster care to some of these children. SCPS is also trying to initiate legal adoption so that these children can be placed in a safe home. In the most recent case, as reported in the local media, involving trafficking of children from Nagaland, the Rajasthan Police rescued 49 children (which included 27 girls from the north-east, aged between 4 and 14) from an illegal orphanage in Jaipur, Rajasthan. The children were kept/confined in shelter homes, which were not registered under government agencies. A man claiming to be a pastor was arrested by police regarding this matter. Police have detained a man identified as Jacob John, who claims to be a pastor, the officer added. According to John, the children are from poor families across the country, particularly from the Punjab, Assam, Manipur, Nagaland and Chhattisgarh.[6]

The 'destination' states of these children were Tamil Nadu, Karnataka, Andhra Pradesh and Kerala. Poor parents were being lured by traffickers with high expectation of quality education for their children. In addition to this, lack of basic infrastructure such as road connectivity, power, hospitals, etc. and insurgency in their local areas led parents to send their children out. More important was the role of middlemen who found it a lucrative business scouting for children from North East to the orphanages in Southern States. Most of such orphanages/homes raised donations against the photographs of children sent to donors. There is no regulation on the activities of the middlemen who arrange and transport children from the North Eastern States on the pretext of free education. There is also little or no check on the illegal/unregistered Children's Homes being run in the Southern Indian States. A lack of regular inspection and surveillance by the Social Welfare/Social Defence authorities, Anti-Human Trafficking Units and local police in the districts/States where these children end up also contributes to the flourishing of these illegal activities. Most of such children are placed in orphanages or Children's Homes that have no registration/recognition from the Government under the Orphanages and other Charitable Homes (Control and Supervision) Act, 1960, or the Juvenile Justice (Care and Protection of Children) Act, 2000. They are placed in crowded buildings, lacking in sanitation facilities, proper food, health care or education. Children are made to cook their food, clean the premises and even subject to abuse. They do not have any contact with their families for over two years or more and soon lose all connection and touch with their mother tongue, culture, community and belonging.

Situation of Trafficking in Manipur

Human trafficking/child trafficking in Manipur is largely related to protracted armed conflict situation in the state[7], ethnic conflict, unregulated migration, using of children as inmates in unrecognized children homes, lack of awareness, lack of communication compounded by poor road connectivity, insurgency, recruitment of children as soldiers in some of the non-state organizations, unequal economic opportunities, opening of the Trans-Asian Highway, prolonged imposition of Armed Forces Special Powers Act, lack of prosecution and conviction of culprits, failure of state mechanism, among others.

Accordingly, we can observe that poor socio-economic condition, bad governance compounded by protracted political armed conflict situation plays a significant role of child (human) trafficking in Manipur. On the other hand, as provided in the reports of the Government officials as well as sources from the local/national media, it is shown that new patterns are also observed in this business (i.e. human trafficking). Either shifting of traditional destination (usually South Indian states) or change of method to lure victims are the common recent trends and patterns for this clandestine business. For instances, earlier, children from Manipur are trafficked in the name of free education, free accommodation and job placement in other Indian states, particularly in the South Indian states. Young girls were also recruited under the pretext of providing training and lucrative job placement in aviation sector, service sector including, beauty parlour, spa industry, domestic help, etc. However, most of these girls are forced to work as sex workers in other Indian states. Today, Manipur has also become a transit route for human trafficking. Traffickers began to recruit young girls from Manipur to be trafficked to South-east Asian countries particularly to Malaysia, Singapore, etc. Young girls are particularly trapped in a false promise of lucrative job in service sector including tourism industry (Niumai, 2016).

Department of Social Welfare, Government of Manipur has rescued and repatriated 379 children and young women from major cities of India, such as Chennai, Bangalore, Delhi and Mumbai during the year 2008 to 2012. They have also been rehabilitated and reintegrated in the society by sending to schools and by providing vocational training in the trade of tailoring and embroidery at the Government Vocational Training Centre at Takyel, Imphal. The year 2008 (October) was a landmark in Manipur while reporting the issues of human trafficking particularly children with the return of 4 girls from Tamenglong District, Manipur and one from Assam, after being trafficked to Singapore and Malaysia for the purpose of sexual exploitation. These girls were recruited by a fake agency through its local based agents by promising jobs in Singapore. It was reported that the traffickers control the victims through a variety of coercive means. In addition to sexual abuse, the traffickers keep their passports, leaving them with few options if they do manage to escape.

Manipur, over the last few years is increasingly known as a source as well as a destination point for trafficking of women and children. It is a deeply entrenched and a growing phenomenon in the conflict prone areas primarily in rural neighbourhood especially the hill districts of Tamenglong, Ukhrul, Chandel, Churachandpur and Senapati. Many of these rescued victims are as young as of seven years who left home when they were 3-4 years old. The figures are not inclusive of all those who were rescued in the transportation process. Exact data of such cases of rescue and repatriation are yet to be disclosed. However, several activists and news reports have consolidated to approximately 300 children victims during the year 2007 to 2010. The highest number of child-trafficking cases in Manipur was recorded in 2010 with as many as 139 children from the state found trafficked to other states in the name of giving free education and jobs. There were cases of 97 trafficked children in 2009, 22 children in 2008 and only five children in 2007. In the month of January, 2010, 54 boys from Tousem sub-division in Tamenglong district were found trafficked to Tamil Nadu and later rescued by the volunteers of Child Welfare Committee (CWC), Tirunelveli from a children home run by one Roman Catholic Missionary, Immanuel Christopher. The boys were admitted to the children home through one local agent, N. Paul from Tamenglong who had taken Rupees 6,000 to Rupees 7,000 from each child with the false promise of giving free education. The boys were kept in miserable conditions with no proper food and education at the children home. It was also reported that the warden of the home also harassed them both mentally and physically. The culprit Immanuel has been jailed but the local agent Paul is still absconding. Another 17 children including eight boys and nine girls from the district of Bishnupur were rescued from Ritz Children Home, Chennai in January. The children were reportedly trafficked to Chennai through local agents, after taking 10,000 Rupees from each child. The girls were sexually harassed at the children home. There was also another case in January, last year in which a 17 years old girl was reportedly trafficked to Tamil Nadu by four women in the name of giving vocational education. Later, the girl was rescued and the culprits were detained under National Security Act (NSA).

In the month of February 2010, three children including two boys and one girl were trafficked to Chennai and later a combined team of CWC Chennai and CWC Bishnupur rescued the children from Ritz Children Home, Chennai. The trafficked children were found in a deplorable condition with clear signs of torture and harassment. The local agent in this case was Miss D from Chandel district. In the month of April 2010, 27 children including 18 girls and 9 boys from Imphal East, Imphal West and Bishnupur were reportedly trafficked to Tamil Nadu by one Henry Ostrin and later rescued by the officials of Social Welfare Department and Child Line Imphal. In the same month, one girl was reportedly trafficked to Chennai as domestic helper by one Angoubi from Lamsang. In the month of May 2010, three boys from Sekta and Keinou were intercepted by CWC Imphal East and Bishnupur at Imphal Tulihal Airport while they were being trafficked to Guwahati by two women in the name of offering job. In the month of June 2010, 12 children including nine boys and three girls were trafficked to Tamil Nadu. In the month of July 2010, 12 children from Bishnupur were trafficked to Chennai by one Herojit from Ithing. Another one girl from Bishnupur was trafficked to Kolkata as domestic worker. In the month of August 2010, four boys from Tamenglong, Imphal East and Imphal West districts were trafficked to Haryana through one Kalyan Ashram, Manipur. In the month of September 2010, three children including two girls and one boy from Churachandpur were trafficked to New Lambulane by the step-mother of the children.

Following reports of rescuing 76 children from Assam and Manipur, being rescued from "homes" run by missionaries in Tamil Nadu, the Supreme Court in the first week of April ordered a probe into a possible trafficking racket involving tribal children. On 1 September, the Supreme Court passed an order that imposes a ban on sending out children below the age of 12 years or those in primary schools to other states to pursue education. The main factor behind parents sending off their ward to other states is for better education at free of cost as promised by the traffickers who are mostly missionaries. Arun Ram from *Times of India* reports that, "the rescue of 76 mal-nourished children, from Manipur and Assam, from a home at Kuzhithurai in Kanyakumari district this week is only the tip of a vast network, which receives crores of rupees from churches and agencies abroad by showing a large number of children under their care." The Court also directed Ministry of DoNER looking after the development affairs of the north-east region to assess requirement in terms of educational infrastructure such as construction of school buildings, hostels and children's homes in consultations with the states of Assam, Nagaland, Manipur, Arunachal Pradesh and Meghalaya and submit a report to the Ministry of Human Resources Development for support.[8]

Concerning the grave situation of child-trafficking in the state, the coordinator of Coalition on Children Right to Protection (CCRP), A. Chinglemba stated that the state government should take up concrete measures to uplift the education system and generate more employment for the youths if the menace of human-trafficking is to be tackled. Mere vigilance of the police and other officials will not help much to counter the problem of trafficking. It is the overall development in socio-economic conditions of the people that will help to reduce the number of human-trafficking cases in the state, he noted. Chinglemba further said that poverty-stricken people are often the victims of human-trafficking and so the government should take up steps to provide them good education and help to generate employment. Failure in education system and the problem of unemployment are the major factors for human-trafficking in Manipur. The magnitude of young non-Manipuri boys and girls frequently seen as child labourers in domestic worker, hotels, restaurants and construction sites need also to be studied extensively.

Movement for Child Rights in Manipur

The situation of child trafficking in Manipur seems to be better as the intervention of the NGOs working on the issues of Child Rights has been very effective. In order to better understand the context, this section will deal with the movement for child rights in Manipur. In this section, the movement undertaken by (i) Coalition on Children's Rights to Protection (CCRP); (ii) Manipur Alliance for Child Rights (MACR); Child Welfare Committees; and (iv) FXB India Suraksa, Manipur will be discussed.

(i) The Coalition on Children's Rights to Protection (CCRP) is a nationwide right based initiative launched by the Child Rights and You (CRY). It was earlier known as the Quality Institutional Care & Alternatives for Children (QIC & AC). It envisages and ensures the rights of child, with special focus on right to protection as enshrined in the CRC of 1989. Some of the important objectives of the CCRP initiatives are:

(a) To understand and mobilize the politics of the people to ensure child rights;
(b) To advocate for realization of human rights as a whole and child rights in particular,
(c) To demand rights from the state actors, and
(d) To build movement collectively through alliance.

The broad long term goals of the CCRP initiatives include prevention of child trafficking, advocacy for proper implementation of the JJ Act, 2000 and its Rules, advocacy for transparent and accountable implementation of the Integrated Child Protection Scheme (ICPS) and ensuring right of children to free and compulsory education in the state of Manipur, among others. The Manipur Mahila Kalyan Samittee acts as the state resource organization for the CCRP. The initiative was started in January, 2005 under the nomenclature of the Quality Institutional Care and Alternative for Children, which was later known as the Coalition on Children's Right to Protection (CCRP). A vibrant core group was formed on the 1st March, 2005 comprising members from different walks of life, such as human rights activists, members of CWCs, lawyers, officials of the government departments and the members of CRY. The CCRP aims to investigate and address the issues relating to violation of child such as rights to life, education and health from larger socio-economic-political and cultural perspectives. Its aim is to advocate the policy-makers, the allied system and the civil society organizations for bringing a just and secured society for the children. The CCRP has been working towards strengthening of the Juvenile Justice System and advocacy of different concerned stakeholders, specially, media, police and other state machineries so as to protect child rights issues in the state. It has also been giving emphasis on collection of primary and secondary data and information relating to violations of child rights in the state even by conducting its own fact findings of such violations of child rights. The children home is one of the important institutions which could safeguard and protect rights of those vulnerable groups of children. There are eight children homes in Manipur which have received grant-in-aid from the state government. Delaying of disbursement of such grant by the government has been one of the main stumbling blocks, specially, for maintaining and functioning of such children homes. The CCRP fact finding team visited such children homes to access the situations and conditions of those homes. The team visited the Alengtang children home of Ukhrul district on the 29th January, 2010 and they found that those children living in the home were conditionally sent back to their respective families on the 22nd December, 2009 in the name of vacation for Christmas. That was mainly happened because of the required fund for management of the home was not released by the state government for more than nine months. Such similar condition has also been found in almost all the children homes in the state.

The CCPR fact finding team visited the Kanglatongbi children home situated in Senapati district on the 15th December, 2009. The said home is one of the oldest children homes in the state which was established in 1947. The team found 55 children including 10 girls living in a poorly maintained house. Those children, living in the said house, did not get even morning tea or breakfast except two meals a day. They were also employed in agricultural works so as to help themselves in meeting the required food for the home. They were living in a miserable condition which was in need of immediate attention of the state government. The team along with media persons also went to the Liwa Chaning destitute home of Chandel district to find out the ground realities of the home on the 29th March, 2011. The home was run by the Liwa Chaning Women Society of Chandel district. The secretary of the society informed the team that the society was not in a position to run the home due to shortage of fund and further stated that the Department of Social Welfare, Government of Manipur had not released the funds in time. The team also came to realize that the home was not in a position to maintain the minimum standard for running a home since the institution had only two *Kuccha* houses without fencing, and it could not provide the basic facilities like power supply, toilet facilities and safe drinking water. The Child Welfare Committee of the district even shifted the children of such home to other private run children homes. The CCPR team found that enforcement of the Juvenile Justice (Care and Protection of Children) Act, 2000 and its Rules were not effectively implemented by the concerned authorities, and it also found that grant-in-aid funds to be provided by the government to such children homes, were found inadequate. Most of the staff and managers of homes were also found not aware of the basic things like the child rights, the social audit, the juvenile justice legislations and the ICPS, among others. Child trafficking is an international crime and also a form of gross violation of child rights. Manipur has been an important hotspot of child trafficking issues in the past couple of years. There were many instances of sending child in group to unauthorized children home of different states of India. As reported in print media, altogether 198 children of the state of Manipur were trafficked to other states of India during the period 2007-2010. It is reported by local media that out of 198 children, 57 children were from Tamenglong district, 25 children from Senapati district, 28 children from Chandel district, 1 from Imphal East district, 6 from Imphal West district, 28 from Bishnupur district, 6 from Churachandpur district and 48 from unspecific areas. It was reported in the local media that all 52 children, who had gone to Nagarcoil, Kannyakumari district of Tamil Nadu, Chennai for obtaining good quality and proper education, have reached their home at Tamenglong district headquarter. The narration of a 15 year old child victim was also reported as "We were made to dig the mud, carrying stones and cleaning toilets with bare hands, if we disobeyed we were beaten up and giving punishment of not giving sufficient foods and place to sleep."

The CCRP visited Chandel district on the 16th February, 2010 and met the chairperson of the CWC, Chandel. The chairperson told the team that 25 children were trafficked from the district to other states of India during 2008 to 2010. Out of them 22 children were rescued with the intervention of the NGOs and the CWC, Chandel from an unauthorized children home run by the Life Trust located near Chennai, Tamil Nadu. The children were said to be ill-treated, harassed and no proper education and adequate food were provided at the home. They were handed over to their families in 2008. Police did not take up any criminal case against the culprits involved in the said commission of the crime.

Human trafficking, particularly, child trafficking has become a common issue in Manipur. It is a heinous crime under national and international laws for which criminal proceeding must be initiated by the concerned departments, government of Manipur against those involved in child trafficking cases. However, the government departments seem to be reluctant to initiate such proceeding against the criminals involved in the cases, that is why, there are no such instances of arrest and punishment of those erring offenders. Lack of awareness, ill effects of child trafficking, displacement, poverty and unavailability of good institutions are some of the major factors for occurrence of such cases of child trafficking in Manipur.

(ii) Manipur Alliance for Child Rights (MACR): MACR was formed on the 23rd December, 2005 by some like minded Community Based Organizations (CBOs) and the non-governmental organizations to create a common platform where issues relating to child rights could be highlighted. The vision of the MACR is to bring about a just society by creating a safe and supportive environment, wherein children's right to life, growth and expression are not denied. The MACR is supported by the Child Rights and You (CRY) since 2006. The organisation has six specific objectives:

(a) To build up linkage or support base from people, NGOs and women groups to ensure the rights of children;
(b) To link with government and pressure groups;
(c) To transform the society to bring about a child friendly environment;
(d) To build up people mobilization process such as pressure groups to ensure rights of children;
(e) To seek solidarity from other peace building movement to integrate holistic child rights by promoting interdependence;
(f) To incubate and mobilize people centred advocacy process against human rights violation in order to ensure child rights.

The MACR has opened its district chapters in Imphal East, West, Thoubal, Bishnupur, Ukhrul and Chandel districts of Manipur. It organized public meetings and rallies in Imphal to protest against increase of crime against child in the state. Right to Education is one of the basic rights of a child which is recognized by both international and national laws. The MACR organized a three day state level discussion on educational status in Manipur at Hotel Imphal on the 27th to 29th July, 2009. The three day discussion recommended to the state government to adopt a comprehensive and holistic state educational policy to meet the emerging challenges of the modern time educational needs and requirements and to cater to the specific needs of the children of Manipur, affected and infected by HIV/AIDS and armed conflict and to provide the specific needs of the disabled child and to declare educational areas as free zones, exempted from bandh and blockade, among others. The MACR believes that proper and timely implementation of Right to Education Act, 2009 by the concerned authorities can bring a phenomenal change in human capital, and it can also minimize the number of school dropout children. The most volatile issues of the children of this state, such as child trafficking, child labour and child soldiering, could also be controlled to a large extent. The MACR not only carried out wide range of poster campaign on right to education for children at Imphal East, Imphal West, Thoubal, Ukhrul, Bishnupur and Chandel districts of Manipur but also organized consultative meetings, workshops and press conferences, specially, to sensitise the people about right to education for children in the state.

The MACR organized a Children Cultural Meet at Manipur Dramatic Hall (MDU), Imphal on the 25th July, 2010 to provide a space for children to enable them to express their understanding and feelings and to release their traumatic experiences in a constructive way. The children of this conflict-ridden state have been found encountering constant fear psychosis trauma that have often led to mental depression. The MACR also visited to six districts of Manipur to access the ground realities of the prevailing situations of children in the remote areas, and they also held meetings, workshops trainings at district levels with the aim to make the common people aware of child rights. Many perspective building workshops were held at Ukhrul, Chandel, Bishnupur, Imphal West and Thoubal districts of Manipur in 2009. Such workshops, conducted in different parts of the state, gave emphasis on issues like armed conflict, ethnic conflict, HIV/AIDS, education, child trafficking and child labour, among others. The activities of MACR have been focusing on pertinent issues relating to protection of right to life and right to education of children in both valley and hill areas of Manipur.

The MACR submitted a memorandum to the NCPCR team headed by Mrs. Dipa Dixit, member of the NCPCR who had visited Manipur on the 24th May, 2011. The memorandum urged upon the NCPCR to recommend the state government in order to expedite the process for setting up a state commission for protection of child rights and to enact an effective legislation to combat human and child trafficking. The memorandum further urged to strengthen criminal justice system and to probe the child trafficking cases effectively by prosecuting the culprits and to adopt a comprehensive state policy for prevention, rescue and rehabilitation planning for child trafficking in the state. The MACR in association with the CRY organized a state level consultation programme on children's right to protection in Imphal on the 7th April, 2012. It recommended to the state government to strengthen the statutory institutions established under the Juvenile Justice (Care and Protection of Children), Act 2000.

(iii) Child Welfare Committee (CWC): The Government of Manipur has established the Child Welfare Committees (CWCs) for every district of the state in the year 2007 in accordance with the provisions of the Juvenile Justice (Care and Protection of Children) Act, 2000. However, even though the members of various CWCs in the state of Manipur are keen to work for children, they are not in a position to function properly because of various factors such as untimely release of fund, lack of necessary support staff and having no permanent office of CWCs lack of Shelter/Children Homes for both boys and girls of all categories including Special Needs Children like HIV/AIDS infected and affected, POCSO victims, mentally retarded, mentally ill, physically challenged, similar and separate special needs institutions for 0-6 years age group. Despite having such limitations, CWCs in Manipur has played a proactive role in rescuing victim of child trafficking from various parts of the country in coordination with the social welfare department, Government of India and CWCs of concerned state from where children of Manipur state has been rescued. The Government of Manipur has, with a view to combating human trafficking, established Anti-Human Trafficking Unit in four districts. The government has also set up Juvenile Police Unit as per the provision of Juvenile Justice (Care and Protection of Children) Act, 2015 which shall be instrumental in combating and preventing child trafficking in the country. However, people are not well aware of having such unit in the police stations.

(iv) FXB India Suraksa, Manipur has recently started a project for combating child trafficking in Manipur. The project has formally been launched in 2015 in Ukhrul district of Manipur. The organisation has started organizing training programmes in Imphal West and Ukhrul districts for stakeholders of various government departments particularly the functionary of social welfare department, members of CWCs, JJBs and media persons relating to laws dealing with child trafficking, causes and consequences of child trafficking.

Conclusion

The existing trend of large number of children being trafficked towards these cities, inspite of the interventions by the NGOs and Government bodies has caught the attention of the Apex Court in India in the form of a PIL. As a result, the state, besides Assam being the respondents, have been directed by the Hon'ble Supreme Court of India vide its order dated 1.09.2010 in the matter of Exploitation of Children in Orphanages in the state of Tamil Nadu vs. UOI and Others concerning large scale transportation of children from one state to another to *ensure that no child below the age of 12 years or those at primary school level are sent outside for pursuing education to other states until further orders.*

The situation is now alarming as the government intervention is also weakening mainly because of lack of seriousness by the government. As discussed earlier, the members have not been paid for more than a year. At the sametime, the activities of the NGOs have also weakened because of the lack of funding. Thus it has become a fertile ground for trafficking. Moreover, James Khagenbam[9] (2012) observed that the grass root level awareness like imparting basic knowledge on trafficking to ignorant citizens in the far flung areas was missing like 'the trafficked kids. The main area of prevention was void in the programmes. The awareness level is not up to the mark in this area. The tributaries of flowing knowledge on trafficking have not reached the high hills and the plain-ends. Knowledge on hazards of trafficking and the way to curb it from a vulnerable state like Manipur should be imparted at the nearest time. Else the count by the profiting criminals as to how many child births take place a day in the state will go on.

Reference

1. Press Information Bureau, Ministry of Home Affairs (2015), Shri Rajnath Singh inaugurates National Conference on Anti-Human Trafficking, 07 October, 2015.
2. See, Paresh. (2015). *A Regional Consultation on Child Trafficking from and into 8 North Eastern States of India 2014-15.* National Commission for Protection of Child Rights (NCPCR), Government of India, North East Cell. New Delhi.

3. Hannah, G. *et al., India's Human Trafficking Laws and Policies and the UN Trafficking Protocol: Achieving Clarity.* Kolkata: Jindal Global Law School.
4. National Commission for Protection of Child Rights (No Date), *Concept Note: A Regional Consultation on Child Trafficking from and into 8 North Eastern States of India, 2014-15,*
5. For details, see Bhattacharjee, S. (2016, April 16). *Why is Meghalaya Vulnerable Towards Crime of Human Trafficking?.* Retrieved January 8, 2017 from neLive: http://www.nelive.in/meghalaya/opinion/why-meghalayavulnerabletowardscrimehumantrafficking0
6. Nagaland State Social Welfare Board (2013). *Consultative Meeting on Combating Human Trafficking in Nagaland.* Kohima: The Nagaland State Social Welfare Board.
7. Also see, Ghosh, A.K. (n.d.). *Child Rights Protection in Manipur Context.* Retrieved October 10, 2016 from CRY—Child Rights and You.
8. James Khagenbam (2012), Child Trafficking: Many rescued yet dozens of minor traceless since 2010 (three Parts) *The Sangai Express* (July 31, 2012, August 08, 2012 October 07, 2012).

3

State of Child Trafficking in Manipur

Methodology of the Study

The study aims to identify the root causes and modus operandi of Child Trafficking. It also aims at finding out the status of child trafficking in Manipur and the initiatives taken by the state agencies. The need of the study arisen is because of the fact that Manipur, in particular and North East India in general, are also one of the sources, transits and destinations for women and child trafficking, especially for sexual exploitation, prostitution and child labour. The region has been a fertile ground for human trafficking for various reasons such as armed conflict, ethnic tension, lack of development and job opportunity and illiteracy. The issue of trafficking seems to be increasing despite the intervention by the government by way of constituting (i) State Level Committee to Combat Human Trafficking chaired by the Chief Secretary, Government of Manipur; (ii) Anti Human Trafficking Units in all the districts by the state Home Department (under the guidelines of the Ministry of Home Affairs, Government of India (GoI); (iii) Anti-Trafficking Squads at the State and District level by the Department of Social Welfare, Government of Manipur; and (iv) Grant-in-Aid given to NGOs for prevention, rescue and rehabilitation of trafficking victims. For instance, MHA Anti-Human Trafficking, UNODC Country Assessment Report on Anti-Human Trafficking, 2013 and other available sources on Child Trafficking examined by NCPCR (2015) revealed that North East India has emerged as a high source area for trafficking of women and children. However, there are very limited studies in trying to understand the issue through a multidisciplinary approach in Manipur except few seminars/conferences/workshops by concerned government agencies and NGOs involved in this issue. It is in this regard, the study was undertaken to analyse and examine the data compiled by the Department of Social Welfare, Government of Manipur. The study will help to anticipate ways and means to effectively combat child trafficking in Manipur. In order to respond to the objectives, the study followed the combined methodological approach of quantitative methodology supplemented by qualitative methodology. It was an exploratory research design.

The data for the study was mainly based on the official compilation of the Department of Social Welfare, Government of Manipur. There are two sets of data or rather two ways of documenting the data of child trafficking in Manipur. The first data set is a compilation of the period from 2008 to 2013 (August) with 486 reported children of trafficking from 39 cases. The second data set is the compilation of the period from 2013 (23 November) – 2016 (26 June) with 80 reported of children trafficking from 5 cases. Since the pattern of documentation was different, the two data sets could not be developed as one single data set for the study. So, for the purpose of the study, the first data set was used as it has more scope to examine the cases than the second data set. Besides, the number of cases in the second data set was very less as compared to the first data set. This does not mean that the first data set is perfect for the study. It has a number of limitations particularly in developing individual profiles of the traffic victims and other socio-economic parameters. The major limitation of the study which we feel is the inability to visit the victims and their families to fill the gap in the documentation developed by the department. We did try to visit the victims and their family members but we came to know that the follow up by the department particularly the concerned CWC was very weak as the CWCs (past and present) were functioning with the limited basic office infrastructure. Thus, we drop the plan as it will be a difficult task to locate the victims and at the same time, we are not sure of the feasibility of interviewing them. So, we mostly concentrated on the government compiled data supplemented by the qualitative interviews. Thus, the findings were presented in simple frequency tables as there is limited scope for statistical analysis. However, the study incorporates the data from the second data set, whenever it gets the opportunity. The table and figures which are developed by combining the two data sets were specifically marked 2008-2016 along with the name of the tables and figures. Besides, a note is also given to understand the table and figure easily.

In order to supplement the data, interviews with open-ended questions were conducted with various stakeholders such as victim families, child rights based NGOs; child rights activist, civil society activist, government official dealing with the issues of child, police officials, member of CWCs, JJBs and MCPCR etc. The stakeholders were indentified through purposive and snowballing sampling method. The method of saturation point will be used to discontinue the data collection process for the qualitative process.

However, it may be because of the sensitivity of the issues or may be because of its possible linkage with the conflict situation, many of the stakeholders/respondents who were consented to interview or to respond the questionnaires later declined or not responded in spite of repeated reminders by our team. Since it was a time-bound study, it was later decided to drop the respondents. We later realised that it was not only the sensitivity of the situation but also the lack of documentations as there is no permanent structure for CWCs and thus it was very difficult for them to respond to the questions. Besides, untimely-payment of the honorariums and other components for more than a year for the past and present chairpersons and members of CWCs and JJBs was also one of the major factors for the lack of response to the study.

State of Child Trafficking

Table 3.1 indicates that 135 children rescued in the year 2010 has been the highest reported case of child trafficking in Manipur. But, the cases reported from the year 2011 till 2013 is a concern and also alarming as the number of cases are all above 100 except 2011. This is alarming because the situation has to be read with the background that the state mechanism to combat trafficking has already put in place particularly by the Department of Social Welfare and Department of Home, Government of Manipur. Besides, the child welfare committees which are constituted under

Table 3.1: Rescued Children from Trafficking 2008-2016 (26 June)

S. No.	Year	No. of Rescued Children
1	2008	45
2	2009	45
3	2010	135
4	2011	53
5	2012	101
6	2013	107
7	2014	00
8	2015	03
9	2016	41
	Total	**530**

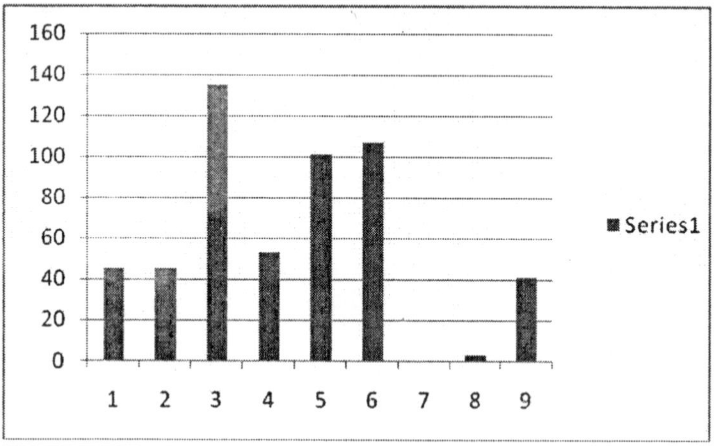

Note: 00 = Data Not Available. This table figure is compiled from two data sources compiled by Department of Social Welfare, Government of Manipur.

the JJ Act were already in operation since 2007 in all the districts of Manipur.

Though, there are indications that the case of trafficking is minimizing in the year 2015, but it again shows concern as it is nearly fifty by June 2016. The sudden fall in the year 2014 and 2015 raise various questions from various quarters as how it can suddenly arrest or control the issue of trafficking. As of now, there is no convincing answer but there is a possibility that it could be a question of under reportage. The question could be because of the fact that the Department does not have a dedicated system for documentation. It seems to be responsibility of the concern officer to document the cases and also to develop the format for documentations. This can be easily verified when we examined the two sets of data which have different format of documentation. The department should discourage the practice of multiple formats and make sure that the documentation system is systematic so that every officer joining the position continues the same process.

Table 3.2: Number of Victims of Child Trafficking

	Sl. No.	*Year of Child Trafficking*					
		2008	*2009*	*2010*	*2011*	*2012*	*2013*
No. of Victims	1	05	25	01	06	40	07
	2	18	04	19	01	21	23
	3	22	16	12	02	07	31
	4			02	19	02	10
	5			55	05	03	36
	6			10	01	04	
	7			09	08	23	
	8			27	02	01	
	9				02		
	10				01		
	11				06		
	12				00		
		45	**45**	**135**	**53**	**101**	**107**
		Grand Total		**486**	**Four Hundred Eighty Six**		

Note: 00 = Data Not Available.

Table 3.2 the description of the number of reported incidents and the reported number of rescued/trafficked children from Manipur. As indicated, there are only eight incidents of trafficking in the year 2010 but it has the highest in terms of children trafficked (135). The incident as well as the number of trafficked children for the year 2008 and 2009 was reported to be same. But, it is observed by child activist that the year 2008 and 2009 should not be considered as good years. It may be because of the lack of documentation either with the government or with the NGOs working on issues of trafficking. Unfortunately, there was no NGO exclusively focusing on child trafficking as it was clubbed under the issue of child rights.

In the year 2011, as compared to the subsequent years, the number of trafficked children is less (53), but, the number of incidents is the highest (11). As disclosed by child activist during field work, it could be a strategy to break down on the number of incidents by the traffickers, as any attempt to continue with the present process (trafficking in large number) can be easily noticeable. So, they might have concentrated on the small number for trafficking. But, in the subsequent year, i.e. 2013, even though the number of incidents is less (05) than 2012 (08), the number of trafficked children is more than 2012 (101) and 2013 (107). So, considering the pattern, there is a possibility that the target for Manipur is to traffic a minimum of hundred children per year. The target seems to have achieved so far as the government intervention particularly by the Department of Home and Department of Social Welfare is not very effective. Likewise, the interventions by the NGOs are also weakening because of the lack of financial support.

Table 3.3: Place of Residence of the Victim

Sl. No.	*Place of Residence*	*Frequency*	*Per cent*
1.	Manipur	31	79.5
2.	Outside Manipur	8	20.5
	Total	**39**	**100.0**

Table 3.3 indicates that the majority i.e. 31 (79.5 %) of the rescued victims are reported to be from Manipur, while only 08 (20.5%) are from other states of India particularly from North East India. What is important in this table is that Manipur is not only a source as assumed by many, where majority of the children are being trafficked to different cities and even to foreign countries, it is also reported to be one of the destinations where children from other states are trafficked for different purposes. There are reports of illegal children homes in Chandel District of Manipur similar to those Illegal homes of Tamil Nadu, which is considered as the main destination of Manipur's trafficked children. These homes are in constant need of children to increase their capacity and thereby chances of increasing their financial support. However, it can be noted that Illegal homes can be managed only with illegal funds, so, there may be a nexus or a cartel for illegal fund or what we call Black Money.

Besides, Manipur being a source as well as a destination, it can be learnt from the report that it is also a 'transit' point where the children are trafficked to other places including foreign countries mainly in Singapore through Myanmar viz-a-viz Moreh of Manipur, which is the gateway to South East Asia. It can be noted that the route to Moreh and to Myanmar is also the Asian Highway No. 1.

Table 3.4: District wise (Manipur) Reported Incidents of Trafficking 2008-2016 (26 June)

Sl. No.	*District*	*No. of Incident*	*Per cent*
1	Imphal West	6	9.09
2	Imphal East	6	9.09
3	Thoubal	2	3.03
4	Bishnupur	8	12.12
	Total	**22**	**33.33**
5	Tamenglong	8	12.12
6	Ukhrul	13	19.69
7	Churachandpur	9	13.63
8	Chandel	8	12.12
9	Senapati	6	9.09
	Total	**44**	**66.66**
	Grand Total	**66**	**100**

Note: Data Not available for 2014. This table with figure is compiled from two data sources compiled by Department of Social Welfare, Government of Manipur.

There are altogether 66 reported incidents of child trafficking in Manipur during the period of 2008-2016 (till June 26) and in that 44 incidents are reported to be from the five hill districts of Manipur whereas only 22 incidents are reported from the four districts of Imphal valley.

The larger number of incidents reported in the five hill districts is because of the fact that the main strategy to lure the family members or relatives by the agent or the person or institutions responsible to recruit the children are mostly for free education facilities and more particularly religious enrichment (read as Christianity). This is relevant as the people of the five hill districts predominantly practice Christianity. So, the entry point in the villages was through Christianity and possibly through the institution of churches which is one of the power centres of the village. This way, they easily get the required trust and confidence on the one hand and security to execute their operation as the institution of churches is deeply respectable by the followers. This may not be true in all cases but it has been confirmed that the religious institutions (Christianity) directly or indirectly plays a major role in trafficking in the hill districts of Manipur. Besides, if we look from a different angle, it could also be seen that the seed of hatred towards the major communities, by instigating that the failure of the school education system is due to the intervention of these communities. In other words, the share for their community is taken away by the major communities inhabiting in the respective district headquarters and more so in the Imphal city.

Considering the gravity of the situation, the Supreme Court of India[1] has ordered a probe into the suspicions growing out of the involvement of missionaries in trafficking innocent tribal children, a majority of them minor girls, from the north-east to southern states. This issue has also been confirmed by President of All Manipur Christian Organization (AMCO) Rev Prim Vaiphei during a consultation meet on child trafficking for pastors, when he stated that some self-styled church functionaries were involved in human trafficking cases.[2]

What is more surprising is that maximum incidents (13) of trafficking amongst the hill districts of Manipur was reported from Ukhrul District, which is dominantly inhabited by Tangkhul Nagas, which is one of the most advance tribal groups in Manipur and North East India in general. The district also has the most vibrant civil societies including human rights groups and traditional institutions at all levels. Tangkhul Naga Long, the apex body of the Tangkhul Nagas is considered to be the backbone of Naga movement in Manipur and Nagaland. In addition, it is also the epicentre for the NSCN (IM) movement and also the birth place of its core functionaries including General Secretary, Th. Muivah.

In terms of literacy also, the district literacy level is very high (81.4%), second only to Churachandpur (82.8%) in terms of hill districts of Manipur. It is fourth rank only to Imphal West (86.1%) the capital of Manipur, Churachandpur (82.8%), and Imphal East (81.9%). The Tangkhul Nagas are the pioneers among the tribes of North East India. For instance, people of Ringui (Tongou) village, a village in Ukhrul district has formally resolved to allow the women to be elected to the village council, which has been the domain of the males so far.

The second place in terms of child trafficking, after Ukhrul district, is Churchandpur district (9), which has the highest literacy among the hill districts and second only to Imphal West in terms of state level. Unlike Ukhrul, where Tangkhul Naga dominates the district, Churachandpur is inhabited by multiple ethnicities particularly from Chin-Kuki-Mizo groups and thus multiple civil societies. It is considered to be the core of the armed movement for Chin-Kuki-Mizos and on the other side; the district has produced the highest number of administrators and police officers. For instance, Manipur police department is presently dominated by Chin-Kuki-Mizos particularly from Churachandpur including the Director General of Police. It was also observed during field-work that the multiplicity of ethnicity and conflict situation among ethnic groups that disturb the livelihoods could be one of the main reasons for trafficking. Besides, there are reports that the ethnic groups (which have similar ethnic background) from Myanmar particularly from Chin-Kuki-Mizos, are also migrating to Churachandpur, mostly with the sole intention of earning a livelihood and thus could be the prospective victims.

In such a scenario, to traffic either children or women will be a difficult task but, in reality children are being trafficked frequently. So, we can assume that there is a nexus with some leaders as well as with the related institutions in the trafficking process particularly by giving a safe passage to the traffickers or in getting approval of the respective CWCs or in introducing them to the prospective villages. There is also report from the Manipur Commission for Protection of Child Rights, that some prominent civil society groups are also involved in getting the CWC approval, in the recent case of child trafficking (100 children), which was rescued from Tamil Nadu (2016) (*see* Table 4.5).

As discussed earlier in Table 4.3, the number of reported victims was 08, but with the addition of the second data set, it comes to 09 numbers of victims. The additional victim is reported to be from Assam. This table verifies that Manipur is not only a destination but also a transit point. We are not sure how many of the victims who are rescued in Manipur are meant for trafficking to other places. The victims are mostly from Eastern India and more particularly North East India. However, with the limitation of cases, no inferences could be drawn from the table except the confirmation of being a destination and a transit and a source for trafficking.

Table 3.5: State-wise (Outside Manipur) Reported Incidents of Trafficking 2008-2016 (26 June)

Sl. No.	*State*	*No. of Incident*	
1.	Assam	4	Hojai, Karimganj, Nalbari & Golaghat
2.	Orissa	1	Berhampur
3.	Meghalaya	1	Ri-Bhoi
4.	Bihar	1	Samastipur
5.	Nagaland	1	Dimapur
6.	Sikkim	1	No Data
	Total	**9**	

Note: Data Not available for 2014. This table with figure is compiled from two data sources compiled by Department of Social Welfare, Government of Manipur.

Table 3.6: Place of Rescue

Sl. No.	*Place of Rescue*	*Frequency*	*Per cent*
1	No Date	3	7.7
2	West Bengal	1	2.6
3	Manipur	19	48.7
4	Karnataka	3	7.7
5	Tamil Nadu	6	15.4
6	Maharashtra	1	2.6
7	Haryana	1	2.6
8	Kerala	2	5.1
9	Rajasthan	2	5.1
10	Uttar Pradesh	1	2.6
	Total	**39**	**100.0**

Table 3.6 indicates that only 48.7 per cent of the cases of rescued children were reported from different parts of Manipur but the majority of the cases (51.3%) were reported from outside the State of Manipur. And out of 51.3 per cent cases reported, 28.2 per cent of the cases are reported only in South India particularly Tamil Nadu (15.4%), Karnataka (7.7%) and Kerala (5.1%). The remaining covers the different regions of India such as Eastern (West Bengal), Western (Maharashtra), Northern (Haryana), Central (Uttar Pradesh) and North Western (Rajasthan) etc. This indicates the increasing demand for trafficked children in India. They might have been rescued during their transit phase to other parts of India

as well. There might be a nexus of illegal children homes, where they circulate the children to other illegal children homes after keeping them for a certain period of time to get their illegal fund or satisfy their needs.

The situation presented in the table also clearly indicates that the traffickers were successful to traffic children in spite of the several layers of stringent state actions and machineries to combat trafficking. The state machineries were supplemented from time to time by the NGOs working on the issues of child rights. But the activities of NGOs were mostly of temporary in nature and could not sustain the movement.

The lack of interest and commitment by the State to combat child trafficking is the opportunity rather a springboard for the traffickers. For instance, the present state government has not been able to locate even a permanent office infrastructure since the inception of the Child Welfare Committees (CWC). The office of the CWCs of Manipur has often been shifting, whenever the new members are appointed. What is more unfortunate is that the State Government has not been able to pay the honorarium of the chairperson and its members for the last few years (this includes former members too). Besides, the non-release of maintenance support such as room rent for the Office of Child Welfare Committees has compelled some of the district CWCs to vacate the rented office.

Besides, the state level anti-trafficking squad formed under Department of Social Welfare to combat the human trafficking is not known to the public—as about the composition of members, its activities and the outcomes so far.[3] The situation of the Juvenile Police Unit is also the same. The main problem with them is that they are assigned with numerous tasks apart from their primary assignments and thus the issue of trafficking probably becomes secondary.

The logic is simple, if the State machinery is sincere and committed; then, most of the cases of rescues of trafficking should have been reported from Manipur and not the other way round.

Table 3.7 indicates that South India particularly Tamil Nadu with 33.3 per cent is shown as one of the favourite destinations for the trafficked children of Manipur. It is closely followed by Karnataka (7.7%) and Kerela (5.1%). What we need to note here is that the so-called destination as reported may not necessarily be

Table 3.7: Destination of the Trafficked Children

Sl. No.	*Destination*	*Frequency*	*Per cent*
1	Manipur	7	17.9
2	Tamil Nadu	13	33.3
3	Singapore	1	2.6
4	West Bengal	1	2.6
5	Karnataka	3	7.7
6	Kerala	2	5.1
7	Rajasthan	2	5.1
8	Uttar Pradesh	2	5.1
9	Haryana	1	2.6
10	Maharashtra	1	2.6
11	Myanmar	1	2.6
12	No Data	5	12.8
	Total	**39**	**100.0**

final destination. For instance, Manipur, albeit considered to be one of the destinations is also found to be a transit point, as one of the rescued victims reveals that they are planning to go further to Myanmar and finally to Singapore. This should be taken seriously as the route of trafficking to Singapore was reported to be through Kolkata via Guwahati and Nagaland. But from the study, we have found that the route has changed recently, i.e. to reach Singapore, Manipur and Mandalay are reported to be the transit points. These reports are further strengthened by the arrest of a lady at Kakching in Thoubal District while trying to traffic three girls to Myanmar on 11 August, 2016 by the Thoubal District Police.

Table 3.8: Rescued from Unauthorised Children Home and No. of Children Rescued

Sl. No.	*Rescued from Unauthorised Children Home*	*Frequency*	*Per cent*	*No. of Children*	*Per cent*
1.	Rescued from Tamil Nadu	6	42.9	151	54.51
2.	Rescued from Rajasthan	2	14.3	30	10.83
3.	Rescued from Uttar Pradesh	1	7.1	03	01.08
4.	Rescued from Karnataka	3	21.4	51	18.41
5.	Rescued from Kerala	1	7.1	23	08.30
6.	Rescued from Maharashtra	1	7.1	19	06.85
	Total	**14**	**100.0**	**277**	**100.00**

It was reported during the analysis of the study that children were mostly rescued from different quarters but rescuing from unauthorised children homes was very prominent. Tamil Nadu tops the number with 42.9 per cent of the unauthorised homes reported in the study, followed by Karnataka (21.4%) and Rajasthan (14.3%). In terms of number of children rescued, 151 children (54.51%) were reported only from the State of Tamil Nadu. The situation indicates that there might be a strong nexus among the traffickers based in Tamil Nadu and some trafficking agents based in Manipur. As indicated earlier, most of the traffickers mask themselves as missionaries or cover themselves as a Good Samaritan of free education that makes difficult to identify and punish the traffickers.

Table 3.9: Case of Unauthorised Children Homes in Tamil Nadu

Sl. No.	*Year*	*No. of Children*	*Place of Residence*
1.	2008	22	Chandel
2.	2009	16	Bishnupur
3.	2010	19	Bishnupur, Imphal East and Imphal West
4.	2010	12	Bishnupur
5.	2010	55	Tamenglong and Chandel
6.	2010	27	Imphal East and Imphal West
	Total	**151**	

Table 3.9 is a breakup of the unauthorised children homes in Tamil Nadu where maximum cases of trafficking are reported and at the same, the maximum numbers of children are rescued so far. This table also shows the place of residence of the trafficked children and in that children were reported from six districts of Manipur except Churachandpur, Senapati and Ukhrul. The year 2010 was also the year with the maximum number of child trafficking (135 children). Considering the gravity of the situation, the state witnessed a big movement for child rights. So, the case of unauthorised children homes was reduced to a great extent but again it seems to be coming back with the rescued for more than 100 children in the year 2016. The children are now rescued by the State Government through the Manipur State Commission for Protection of Child Rights and Child Welfare Committees.

Another interesting revelation in the table was that Ukhrul and Churachandpur did not figure in these years (see Table 3.4), but in the later years Ukhrul and Churachandpur were reported to be first and second in terms of incidents of trafficking in the five hill districts of Manipur. This also shows that the traffickers have changed their strategy to recruit children and in the selection of districts.

Table 3.10: Conditionality of Trafficking

Sl. No.	*Conditions*	*Frequency*	*Per cent*
1.	Free School Education and Boarding	22	56.4
2.	Employment	11	28.2
3.	Skill Training	3	7.7
4.	No data	3	7.7
	Total	**39**	**100.0**

Table 3.10 indicates that the families and relatives of the trafficked children were lured, rather convinced with free school education and free boarding (56.4%) plus Employment (28.2%) and Skill Training (7.7%). This indicates that the trafficker seems to have studied and understood the traffic scenario of Manipur and more particularly at the local level from where they are planning to recruit children. This also helps them (traffickers) to understand the priority of the families and their (parent's) inability to fulfil the priority. Thus, school education tops the condition for trafficking as the importance and influence of education has been an issue all-over particularly in the community level institutions such as churches. At the same time, the traffickers seem to have exploited the failure of government school education in Manipur. For instance, the government run schools as well as the autonomous district schools are mostly ineffective in providing school education. This could probably be the reason why the most literate districts, i.e. Churachandpur and Ukhrul top the list of incident in the hill districts of Manipur. This has landed many of the children in unauthorised children homes and unrecognised schools in different parts of India.

Table 3.11: Action Taken by the Government

Sl. No.	*Government Actions*	*Frequency*	*Per cent*
1.	Resorted and Repatriated to the respective parents	32	82.1
2.	Handed over to the concerned CWC of the respective State	6	15.4
3.	No Data	1	2.5
	Total	**39**	**100.0**

As reported, 82.1 per cent of the rescued victims from Manipur are now restored and repatriated back to their families. While 15.4 per cent of the victims particularly from outside the state of Manipur were handed to their respective Child Welfare Committees to be restored and repatriated to their respective parents and to provide the necessary facilities through their respective States. Table 3.11 shows that there is one missing data of one case, as this particular case is found to be restored and repatriated to the respective Child Welfare Committees.

Table 3.12: Rehabilitation Process

Sl. No.	*Facilities*	*Frequency*	*Per cent*
1.	Provided Skills Development Training	4	10.3
2	Provided Shelter and Education Scholarship	2	5.1
3.	Provided Education Scholarship	11	28.2
4.	Provided Counselling to the children and their parents	7	17.9
5.	No data	15	38.5
	Total	**39**	**100.0**

Table 3.12 indicates that 33.3 per cent (Sl. No. 2 & 3) of the rehabilitation process of the government focuses on providing school education. But it is unfortunate to observe that the government are sending back the victims to the government school system of their districts which they considered a failure. So, they are reinstated to "square one" situation after the whole unfortunate process of trafficking and thus the rehabilitation process became a total failure. Moreover, the government has not been able to follow up the case to examine the status of the victims and the benefits of their rehabilitation process.

Table 3.13: Action Taken against the Perpetrator

Sl. No.	Action Taken against the Perpetrator	Frequency	Per cent
1.	FIR filed	13	33.3
2.	The accused could not identified	3	7.7
3.	Destination state has already taken up action against the accused	14	35.9
4.	Sent to the jail	3	7.7
5.	No data	6	15.4
	Total	**39**	**100.0**

Table 3.13 indicates that different actions were taken by the government of Manipur, against the perpetrators of the child trafficking in the form of filing of First Information Report (FIR) with 33.3 per cent and by awarding jail term with 7.7 per cent. And in terms of the traffickers who belong to other states, it was reported that 35.9 per cent of the perpetrators were reported to have taken action against them. But it is not sure what type of actions was taken against them. What we fail to identify in this study is how many of them are out in bail and how many of the cases are not able to proceed any further. It was also revealed by the child activists during interview that, there are a number of limitations in order to take further course of action due to lack of substantial evidence.

The table also indicates that some of the perpetrators (7.7%) of the trafficking cases could not be identified. This is mainly because there are high chances that the traffickers must have successfully convinced them to come on their own way without even making them to realise that they are in the process of trafficking. This motivation could not be done without the personal interaction with the traffickers, who are reported to be mostly missionaries.

Notes

1. Dhananjay Mahapatra (2010), "Missionaries trafficking kids from NE states?", *The Times of India,* Pune.
2. James Khangenbam (2012), "Child Trafficking: Many rescued yet dozens of minor traceless since 2010 (three Parts)", *The Sangai Express* (July 31, 2012, August 08, 2012 October 07, 2012).
3. *Ibid.*

4
Government Interventions and Child Trafficking

This chapter explains the existing provisions in India including Manipur that are related to prevention, protection and promotion of child rights in the context of child trafficking in India. The chapter does not provide the analysis of the provisions but rather provides a glimpse of it as it becomes necessary to understand the relationship between the government interventions and the issues of child trafficking in India. They are closely related as decrease or increase in human trafficking will depend on the effectiveness of government intervention. It begins with the Constitution of India and concludes with the schemes related to the issue of child trafficking.

(a) Constitution of India

Constitution is the supreme law of the land. A constitution states or ought to state not rules for passing hours, but principles for and expanding future.[1] Part III of the constitution of India embodies fundamental rights, which are considered as the conscience of it. The word fundamental means these inherent rights recognized and guaranteed by the fundamental law of the land. Such rights represent the basic value of the civilized society, and the constitution makers declared that they should be given a higher place in the constitution. Article 23 of the constitution prohibits trafficking in human being and other similar forms of forced labour and pronounce that such acts are offences punishable in accordance with law. Article 24 of the constitution also provides that no child, below the age of 14 years, shall be employed to work in any factory or mine or engaged in any other hazardous employment.

The Directive Principles of State Policy contained in the part IV of the constitution of India, plays the major role in the formulation of state policy. The directive principles may be also called the basis on which legislature is built on. The directive principles of state policy envisage the socio-economic rights of the citizens of India. Article 39 of the constitution directs the state to formulate suitable policies of protection and promotion of the health and strength of labourer and workers, women and the tender age children, and therefore the citizens are not forced by the economic necessity to enter a vocation unsuited to their age or strength. It is further provided by the article 37 of the constitution that the state shall direct its policy towards securing that children are given adequate opportunities and facilities to develop in a healthy manner, so that children and the youths are protected against such exploitations. Some of the related articles are listed in the Table 4.1.

(b) Supreme Court

The Supreme Court has been found proactive specially in the cases involving the genuine concern of the poor and helpless masses of the country. If legislature and executive were silent on the issues concerned with such persons the apex court has to step in. Judiciary has actively engaged in translating the fundamental rights of citizens into reality, more particularly after the declaration of national emergency in 1975.

In Vishal Jeet *vs.* Union of India[2], the Supreme Court directed the government to ensure care, protection, development treatment and rehabilitation of victims of commercial sexual exploitation and to set up a central advisory committee in this regard. The Central Government was further directed by the court to look into the inadequacies of the law, system, and institution relating to prevention and prohibition of trafficking in India. In pursuance of the judgement of the Supreme Court, the state governments have also established State Advisory Committees.

In Gaurab Jain *vs.* Union of India[3], the Supreme Court constitutes Mahajan Committee to investigate into the problem of trafficking in human beings and to submit a detailed report along

Table 4.1: Constitutional and Legislative Provisions Related to Trafficking in India[4]

Sl. No.	*Article*	*Provision*
1.	Article 14: Equality before Law	The State shall not deny to any person equality before the law or equal protection of the laws within the Territory of India.
2.	Article 21: Prohibition of discrimination on grounds of religion, race, caste, sex or place or birth	(i) The State shall not discriminate against any citizen on grounds only of religion, race, caste, sex, place of birth or any of them.
3.	Article 21: Protection of life and personal liberty	No person shall be deprived of his life or personal liberty except according to procedure established by law.
4.	Article 21-A: Right to education	The State shall provide free and compulsory education to all children of the age of six to fourteen years in such manner as the State may, by law, determine.
5.	Article 23: Prohibition of traffic in human beings and forced labour	(i) Traffic in human beings and beggars and other similar forms of forced labour are prohibited and any contraventions of this provisions shall be an offence punishable in accordance with law. (ii) Nothing in this article shall prevent the State from imposing compulsory service for public purposes, and in imposing such service the State shall not make any discrimination on grounds only of religion, race or class or any of them.
6.	Article 24: Prohibition of employment of children on factories, etc	No child below the age of fourteen shall be employed to work in any factory or mine or engaged in any other hazardous employment.
7.	Article 39-A: Equal justice and free legal aid	The State shall secure that the operation of the legal system promotes justice, on a basis of equal opportunity, and shall, in particular, provide free legal aid, by suitable legislation or securing justice are not denied to any citizen by reason of economic or other disabilities.

with guidelines for addressing to the issue. The investigation found that a large number of persons who are the victims of prostitution were children.

The Court further observed that segregating children of prostitutes by locating separate schools and providing separate hostels would not be in the interest of the children and the society at large. They would be allowed to mingle with others so that they would become a part of the society.

In a judgement passed by the Hon'ble Supreme Court in Bachpan Bachao Andolan *vs.* Union of India, the Ministry of Home Affairs has issued an advisory order to the Additional Chief Secretaries/Principal Secretaries (Home) of all states and Union Territories to file FIR in case of missing children. The direction includes the following:

(i) In case of complaint with regard to any missing child; made in a police station, the same should be reduced into a First Information Report and appropriate steps should be taken to see that follow up investigation is taken up immediately thereafter.

(ii) In case of every missing child reported; there will be an initial presumption of either abduction or trafficking, unless, in the investigation, the same is proved otherwise.

(iii) Whenever any complaint is filed before the police authorities regarding a missing child, the same must be entertained under Section 154 Cr.P.C. However, even in respect of complaints made otherwise with regard to a child, which may come within the scope of Section 155 Cr.P.C., upon making an entry in the Book to be maintained for the purposes of Section 155 Cr.P.C., and after referring the information to the Magistrate concerned, continue with the inquiry into the complaint.

(iv) The Magistrate, upon receipt of the information recorded under Section 155 Cr.P.C., shall proceed, in the meantime, to take appropriate action under sub-section (2), especially, if the complaint relates to a child and, in particular, a girl child.

(v) Each police station should have, at least, one Police Officer, especially instructed and trained and designated as a Juvenile Welfare Officer in terms of Section 63 of the Juvenile Act. Special Juvenile Officer on duty in the police station should be present in shifts.

(vi) Para-legal volunteers, who have been recruited by the Legal Services Authorities, should be utilized, so that there is, at least, one paralegal volunteer, in shifts, in the police station to keep a watch over the manner in which the complaints regarding missing children and other offences against children are dealt with.

(vii) The State Legal Services Authorities should also work out a network of NGOs, whose services could also be availed at all levels for the purpose of tracing and reintegrating missing children with their families which, in fact, should be the prime object, when a missing child is recovered.

(viii) Every found/recovered child must be immediately photographed by the police for purposes of advertisement and to make his relatives/guardians aware of the child having been recovered/found.

(ix) Photographs of the recovered child should be published on the website and through the newspapers and even on the T.V. so that the parents of the missing child could locate their missing child and recover him or her from the custody of the police.

(x) Standard Operating Procedure must be laid down to handle the cases of missing children and to invoke appropriate provisions of law where trafficking, child labour, abduction, exploitation and similar issues are disclosed during investigation or after the recovery of the child, when the information suggests the commission of such offences.

(xi) A protocol should be established by the local police with the High Courts and also with the State Legal Services Authorities for monitoring the case of a missing child.

(xii) Definition of Missing Child: Missing child has been defined as a person below eighteen years of age, whose whereabouts are not known to the parents, legal guardians and any other person who may be legally entrusted with the custody of the child, whatever may be the circumstances/causes of disappearance. The child will be considered missing and in need of care and protection within the meaning of the later part of the Juvenile Act, until located and/or his/her safety/well being is established.

(xiii) In case a missing child is not recovered within four months from the date of filing of the First Information Report, the matter may be forwarded to the Anti-Human Trafficking

Unit in each State in order to enable the said Unit to take up more intensive investigation regarding the missing child.

(xiv) The Anti-Human Trafficking Unit shall file periodical status reports after every three months to keep the Legal Services Authorities updated.

(xv) In cases where First Information Reports have not been lodged at all and the child is still missing, an F.I.R. should be lodged within a month from the date of communication of this Order and further investigation may proceed on that basis.

(xvi) Once a child is recovered, the police authorities shall carry out further investigation to see whether there is an involvement of any trafficking in the procedure by which the child went missing and if, on investigation, such links are found, the police shall take appropriate action thereupon.

(xvii) The State authorities shall arrange for adequate Shelter Homes to be provided for missing children, who are recovered and do not have any place to go to. Such Shelter Homes or After-care Homes will have to be set up by the State Government concerned and funds to run the same will also have to be provided by the State Government together with proper infrastructure. Such Homes should be put in place within three months, at the latest. Any private Home, being run for the purpose of sheltering children, shall not be entitled to receive a child, unless forwarded by the Child Welfare Committee and unless they comply with all the provisions of the Juvenile Justice Act, including registration.[5]

(c) Statutory Laws

Parliament of India has so far adopted various legislations which can be read and analyzed in the context of human trafficking or the rights of women and children. However, we have examined some iegislation which we feel more relevant and offer direct intervention to the issue of human trafficking. The legislations which are indirectly related as follows.

(i) Indian Penal Code, 1860

Legislation is the pronouncement of the legal rule by the competent authority of state. The commitment of the state to address the problems of trafficking in human beings is found in various laws, enacted by the Government of India. The Indian Penal Code, 1860 contains dozens of provisions dealing with prevention and prohibition of trafficking in women and children and such provisions also impose criminal penalties for commission of such offences, like kidnapping, abduction, buying or selling a person for slavery or buying and selling minor for prostitution. The Criminal Law (Amendment) Act, 2013 amended section 370 of the Indian Penal Code by substituting the said section and provide the definition of the offence of trafficking. It provides that whoever, for the purpose of exploitation (a) recruits, (b) transports, (c) harbours, (d) transfers or (e) receives, a person or persons, by – First, using threat, or Secondly, using force, or any other form of coercion, or Thirdly, by abduction, or Fourthly, by practicing fraud, or deception or Fifthly, by abuse of power, or Sixthly- by inducement, including the giving or receiving of payments or benefits, in order to achieve the consent of any person having control over the person recruited, transported, harboured, received, commits the offence of trafficking. The person who commits the offence of trafficking shall be punished with rigorous imprisonment for a term which shall not be less than seven years, but which may extend to ten years, and shall also be liable to fine. Section 370(5) further states that the quantum of punishment for the offence of trafficking of more than a minor shall not be less than fourteen years, but which may be extended to imprisonment for life, and shall also be liable to fine. Section 366 of IPC provides that whoever induces any woman to go from any place with intent that she may be or knowing that it is likely that she will be forced or seduced to illicit intercourse with another person shall be punishable imprisonments of either description for a term which may extend to ten years and shall also be liable to fine.

Further, section 372 of IPC, 1860 prohibits selling minor for the purpose of prostitution, and section 373 criminalises the act of buying minor for the purpose of prostitution. Importation of any girl under the age of twenty-one years of age to India from outside India is also penal offence under the Indian Penal Code. Section

371 provides that whoever habitually imports, exports, removes, buys, sells, traffic or deals in slaves, shall be punished with life imprisonment, or with imprisonment of either description for a term not excluding ten years and shall also be liable to be fined.

(ii) Immoral Traffic (Prevention) Act, 1956

The Immoral Traffic (Prevention) Act, 1956 is one of the main legislations enacted by the Parliament for preventing and combating trafficking in human beings in India. The law was enacted in pursuance of the International Convention for the Suppression of Immoral Traffic in Person and the Exploitation of the Prostitution of Other, 1950. Initially, the law was enacted as the Suppression of Immoral Traffic in Women and Girls Act, 1956, and the Act was amended twice. The first amendment took place in 1978 and further; it was amended and renamed as the Immoral Traffic (Prevention) Act, 1956. The prime objective of the Act is to abolish trafficking in women and girls, for the purpose of prostitution as an organised means of living. The Act criminalizes procurers, traffickers and profiteers of the trade but in no way it defines trafficking *per se* in human being. However, the Goa Children Act, 2003 defines child trafficking as the procurement, recruitment, transportation, transfer, harbouring, receipt of person, legally or illegally, within or across borders by means of threat or use of the force or other terms of coercion of abduction, of frauds, of deception, of the abuse of power or of a position of vulnerability or of giving or receiving payment of benefits to achieve the consent of the person having control over another person, for monetary gain or otherwise. The maximum punishment that may be inflicted to the offenders under the Immoral Traffic Prevention Act, 1956 is rigorous imprisonment for a term of not less than seven years and not more than 14 years.

(iii) *The Juvenile Justice (Care and Protection of Children) Act, 2015*

The Juvenile Justice (Care and Protection of Children) Act, 2015 is the most comprehensive and self-contained law ever enacted by the Indian Parliament for the promotion and protection of children in the entire country. The Act not only supplements and elaborates the constitutional provisions relating to children as enshrined in various articles of the Part III and IV of the constitution but also reflects India's commitment to fulfil her international obligation arising out of the signing and ratification of international conventions relating to children. The Act has sixteen principles and contains 112 sections. It deals with two categories of child – child in conflict with law and child in the need of care and protection. Victims of child trafficking are included in the category of child in the need of care and protection as defined in section 2(14) of the Act. This category of children are taken care of by the Child Welfare Committee to be established in accordance with section 27 of the JJB Act, 2015 and the power and function of such committee is laid down in the sections 29 and 30 of the Act. The function of Child Welfare Committee includes:

(i) Taking cognizance of and receiving the children produced before it;
(ii) Conducting inquiry on all issues relating to and affecting the safety and well-being of the children under this Act;
(iii) Directing the Child Welfare Officers or probation officers or District Child Protection Unit or non-governmental organizations to conduct social investigation and submit a report before the Committee;
(iv) Conducting inquiry for declaring fit persons for care of children in need of care and protection;
(v) Directing placement of a child in foster care;
(vi) Ensuring care, protection, appropriate rehabilitation or restoration of children in need of care and protection, based on the child's individual care plan and passing necessary directions to parents or guardians or fit persons or children's homes or fit facility in this regard;
(vii) Selecting registered institution for placement of each child requiring institutional support, based on the child's age, gender, disability and needs and keeping in mind the available capacity of the institution;
(viii) Conducting at least two inspection visits per month to the residential places/facilities for children in need of care and protection and recommending action for improvement in quality of services to the District Child Protection Unit and the State Government;

(ix) Certifying the execution of the surrendered deed by the parents and ensuring that they are given time to reconsider their decision as well as making all efforts to keep the family together;

(x) Ensuring that all efforts are made for restoration of abandoned or lost children to their families following due process, as may be prescribed;

(xi) Declaration of orphan, abandoned and surrendered child as legally free for adoption after due inquiry;

(xii) Taking *suo motu* cognizance of cases and reaching out to children in need of care and protection, who are not produced before the Committee, provided that such decision is taken by at least three members;

(xiii) Taking action for rehabilitation of sexually abused children who are reported as children in need of care and protection to the Committee by Special Juvenile Police Unit or local police, as the case may be, under the Protection of Children from Sexual Offences Act, 2012;

(xiv) Dealing with cases referred by the Board under sub-section (2) of section 17;

(xv) Coordinating with the police, labour department and other agencies involved in the care and protection of children with support of the District Child Protection Unit or the State Government;

(xvi) In case of a complaint of abuse of a child in any child care institution, the Committee shall conduct an inquiry and give directions to the police or the District Child Protection Unit or labour department or child line services, as the case may be;

(xvii) Accessing appropriate legal services for children;

(xviii) Such other functions and responsibilities, as may be prescribed. [6]

(iv) Trafficking of Persons (Prevention, Protection, and Rehabilitation) Draft Bill, 2016

The Ministry of Woman and Child Deployment, Government of India, has also formulated a protocol for Pre-Rescue, Rescue and Post-Rescue operation of child victims of trafficking for commercial sexual exploitation in 2005. This protocol contains guidelines for state governments and it also provides for the strategy of Rescue team members for pre-rescue, and post-rescue operations concerning children who are victims of trafficking and found to be sexually exploited for commercial reasons.

The Government of India under the aegis of the Ministry of Women and Child Development has formulated Trafficking of Persons (Prevention, Protection, and Rehabilitation) Draft Bill, 2016 to prevent trafficking of persons and to provide protection and rehabilitation to the victims of trafficking and to create a legal, economic, and social environment against trafficking of persons. The Bill aims at giving effect to the United Nations Convention on Transnational Organised Crime and its three Optional Protocols, including the Protocol to Prevent, Suppress and Punish Trafficking in Persons, especially women and children because India has ratified the said Convention. The Draft Bill contains 40 articles and XII chapters. It provides for the establishment of committees such as District Anti-Trafficking Committee to prevent, rescue, protect and rehabilitate the victims of human trafficking and State Anti-Trafficking Committee in order to oversee the implementation of this Act and advice the state or union territories government and District Anti-Trafficking Committee. The District Anti-Trafficking Committee consists of a chairperson and 4 (four) members out of which one shall be Member Secretary of the committee. Section 3 of the Draft Bill provides that committee is to be composed of the following members, namely:

Sl. No.	*Remark*	*Designation*
1.	District Magistrate or District Collector	Chairperson
2.	Two social workers out of which one shall be a women nominated by the District Judge	Members
3.	One representative from the District Legal Services Authority nominated by the District Judge	Member
4.	District Officer of the Social Justice or Women and Child Development Department of the concerned States/Union Territories	Member-Secretary

The State Anti-Trafficking Committee consists of a Chairperson and 8 (eight) members. Section 5 of the Draft Bill provides that the committee shall be headed by the Chief Secretary as Chairperson and the followings shall be the members of the said committee:

Sl. No.	Remark	Designation
1.	Chief Secretary	Chairperson
2.	Secretary to the Department of State dealing with Women and Child	Member
3.	Secretary of the State, Home Department	Member
4.	Secretary of the State, Labour Department	Member
5.	Secretary of the State, Health Department	Member
6.	Director General of Police of the concern State	Member
7.	Two social workers out of which one shall be a woman and to be nominated by the Chief Justice of the High Court	Members

The Central Anti-Trafficking Advisory Board headed by the Secretary, Ministry of Women and Child Development, is empowered to oversee the implementation of the Act and advise the appropriate government on matters relating to prevention of trafficking, protection and rehabilitation of victims. So, the Draft Bill incorporates three tire implementation systems. Section 15 of the Draft Bill spells out the punishment for disclosure of the identity of the victim of trafficking. It provides that no report, or any newspaper, or magazine, or audio-visual media, or any other form of communication regarding any investigation or judicial procedure shall disclose the name, address, or any other particulars which may lead to the identification of a victim, or witness of a crime of trafficking in persons under this Act, or any other law for the time being in force, nor shall the picture of any such victim be published.

It further provides that the publisher or owner of the media or studio or photographic facilities or any person in-charge of publication who contravenes the provision of sub-section (1) shall be punishable with imprisonment for a term which may be extended to six months or with fine which may be extended to one lakh rupees, or both. The Draft Bill obligates the state governments to specify for each district a Court of Session to be a Special Court for the purpose of providing a speedy trial of offences punishable under sections 370 to 373 of the IPC and offences under the Act. However, the Draft Bill does not define the term human trafficking in any provisions of the Bill even though it is, for the first time, defined in the IPC in accordance with the Criminal Law (Amendment) Act, 2013. It should be mandatory to include such important definition of the term in the definition clause of the Draft Bill.

Table 4.2: Related Legislations in India[7]

Sl. No.	*Legislations*	*Objectives*
1.	The Protection of Children from Sexual Offences Act, 2012 (notified on 14 December 2012)	The Protection of Children from Sexual Offences Act, 2012 has been enacted to strengthen the legal provisions for the protection of children from sexual abuse and exploitation. For the first time, a special law has been passed to address the issue of sexual offences against children. Sexual offences are currently covered under different sections of IPC. The IPC does not provide for all type of sexual offences against children and, more importantly, does not distinguish between adult and child victims. The protection of children from Sexual Offences Act, 2012 defines a child as any person below the age of 18 years and provides protection to all children under the age of 18 years from the offences of sexual assault, sexual harassment and pornography. These offences have been clearly defined for the first time in law. The Act provides for stringent punishments, which have been graded as per the gravity of the offences. The punishments range from simple to rigorous imprisonment of varying periods. There is also provision for fine, which is to be decided by the court.
2.	Immoral Traffic (Prevention) Act, 1956	To combat commercial sexual exploitations and prohibit prostitution. It has provisions for providing rehabilitation and protection to victims of commercial sexual exploitation.
3.	The Juvenile Justice (Care and Protection of Children) Act, 2000	Defines a child and provides provisions for care and protection of children. It has provisions which provide for protection measures for the repatriation and rehabilitation of children.
4.	Child Labour (Protection and Regulation) Act, 1986	It has the provisions which prohibit child labour. The law has provisions for rehabilitation of child labour.

(*Contd.*)

Sl. No.	*Legislations*	*Objectives*
5.	Bonded Labour System (Abolition) Act, 1976	It defines and prohibits Bonded Labour. It has provision for punishment for bonded labour and provides for rehabilitation measures for bonded labour.
6.	Inter-State Migrant Worker (Regulation of Employment Conditions) Act, 1979	It provides institutional machinery to provide safe migration opportunities for labour.
7.	The Goa Children's Act, 2003	The Goa Children Act is a State legislation. The legislation provides for holistic care and protection of children. It also has the definition of human trafficking as per the UN protocol.
8.	Maharashtra Control of Organised Crime Act, 1979	*Interalia* it provides for punishment of persons indulging in organised crime related to prostitutions.
9.	The Immigration Act, 1994	Provides for regulatory mechanism for recruitment agencies and related punishments.
10.	CARA Guidelines	The guidelines provide for mechanism to regulate adoptions. It has provisions to prevent human trafficking through adoptions.
11.	The Criminal Law Amendment Act, 2013	Section 370 of the Indian Penal Code (IPC) has been substituted with new sections, 370 and 370A which deal with trafficking of person for exploitation. If a person (a) recruits, (b) transports, (c) harbour, (d) transfers, or (e) receives, a person by using threats, or force, or coercion, or abduction, or fraud or deception, or by abuse of power, or inducement for exploitation including prostitution, slavery, forced organ removal, etc. will be punishable with imprisonment ranging from at least 7 years imprisonment to the remainder of that person's natural life depending on the number or category of persons trafficked. Employment of a trafficked person will attract penal provision as well.

(d) Anti-Trafficking Cell, Ministry of Home Affairs

Considering the need for combating the crime of human trafficking in India, the Ministry of Home Affairs has established a Nodal Cell for dealing with matters relating to trafficking in human beings. The Cell is, *interalia,* responsible for collecting and analyzing the data related to trafficking from the State Governments/Union Territories' Administrations, identifying problem areas and analyzing causes for their being source/transit/ destination areas, monitoring the action taken by the State Governments/UTs Administrations for combating the crime and organizing coordination meetings with the Nodal Police Officers of States/UTs. Nodal Officers of Anti-Human Trafficking Units have been nominated in all States/UTs and MHA conducts review meetings with these officers periodically.

The Ministry of Home Affairs has sanctioned a Comprehensive Scheme "Strengthening law enforcement response in India against Trafficking in Persons through Training and Capacity Building, wherein it is proposed to establish 330 Anti-Human Trafficking Units (AHTUs) throughout the country and impart training to 10,000 police officers through Training of Trainers (TOTs) component. The Ministry of Home Affairs has already released two instalments in 2010-11 and 2011-12 for establishment of 225 AHTUs to the State Governments. All the AHTUs have been made operational. In 2014, MHA released funds for Rs. 3.41 crores for establishment of 45 more AHTUs to State Governments of Andhra Pradesh, Gujarat, Harayana, Kerala, Nagaland, Odisha, Uttar Pradesh, Uttarakhand, Madhya Pradesh and Mizoram (*see* Table 4.3).[8]

(e) State and Child Rights in Manipur

The intervention of the state of Manipur in relation to rights of the child can be examined in the context of various Commissions and Committees. However, the performances of these Committees and Commissions need to be strengthened and fully supported in terms of manpower and resources by the State Govt. The most active among them is the Child Welfare Committees (CWCs) constituted under the JJ Act, 2000 and amended in 2015. The limitation and status of the commissions and committees will be broadly defined in the section.

(i) Manipur Human Rights Commission, 1998

The Manipur Human Rights Commission (MHRC) was set up in 1998 under section 21 of the Protection of Human Rights Act, 1993

Table 4.3: MHA Advisories[9]

Sl. No.	*Advisory*	*Date*
1.	Advisory on Crime Against Women	04/09/2009
2.	Advisory on Preventing and Combating Human Trafficking in India	09/09/ 2009
3.	Advisory on Crime Against Children	14/07/2010
4.	Advisory on Prevention, Registration and Prosecution of Crime	16/07/2010
5.	Advisory on Preventing Cyber Crime Against Children	16/07/2010
6.	Advisory on Preventing and Combating Human Trafficking during Commonwealth Games.	10/09/2010
7.	Advisory on Missing Children	31/01/2012
8.	Advisory on Human Trafficking – Organised Crime	30/04/2012
9.	Advisory on Human Trafficking – Dealing with Foreign Nationals	01/05/2012
10.	Advisory on Hon'ble Supreme Court's direction to file FIR in case of Missing Children	25/06/2013
11.	SOP to handle trafficking of children for child labour	12/08/2013
12.	Advisory on Anti-Human Trafficking	05/05/2014
13.	Advisory for associating SSB and BSF in crime meeting	23/07/2015

and it had started its function from 10th December, 1998. The Commission not only receives and examines petitions filed by the victims of human rights violations but also takes up *suo motu* cases on alleged violations of human rights including child rights. The MHRC received and admitted 1264 cases of human rights violations in the state since its inception till 4th April, 2010 and disposed of 331 cases so far. It entertained 52 cases relating to violations of child rights during the last ten years i.e., from 6th April 1999, to 7th February, 2009, and out of which, 21 cases were found to be related with crime of rape.[10] However, the commission has been dysfunctional since 2010 because of non-appointment of chairperson and members of the commission.

Recognizing and realizing the national and international obligations for promotion and protection of child rights, Government of India enacted the Commission for Protection of Child Rights Act, 2005. The Act provides for establishment of National Commission for Protection of Child Rights (NCPCR) and State Commission for Protection of Child Rights, both of which are independent and impartial fact-finding statutory bodies. The Act stipulates adequate provisions for speedy trial of offences committed against children.

(ii) Manipur Commission for Protection of Child Rights, 2012

The Government of Manipur had established the Manipur Commission for Protection of Child Rights (MCPCR) on the 2nd November, 2012 under section 17 of the Commission for Protection of Child Rights Act, 2005 with a commitment of effective implementation of promotional and protective rights of child in the state. The MCPCR which consists of a Chairperson and six members from different districts of Manipur had started its functioning from the 12th November, 2012 with its office at Imphal. The Government had also formulated the Manipur Commission for Protection of Child Rights Rules, 2011 which incorporates additional functions of the Commission.[11] Rule 13 of MCPCR stipulates that the Commission shall, in addition to the functions assigned to the commission under clauses (a) to (j) of sub-section (1) of section 13 the National Commission for Protection of Child Rights Act, 2005 perform seven important functions for promotion and protection of child rights. The said Rules provide that the MCPCR shall perform the following functions:

(a) To analyse existing law, policy and practice to assess compliance with Convention on the Rights of Child and undertake inquiries and produce reports on any aspect of policy or practice affecting children and commitment on proposed new legislation from a child rights perspective;
(b) To undertake formal investigations where concern has been expressed either by children themselves or by concerned person on their behalf;
(c) To ensure that the work of the State Commission is directly informed by the views of children in order to reflect their priorities or perspectives;
(d) To promote, and respect serious consideration of the views of children in its work and that of all Government departments and organizations dealing with child;
(e) To produce and disseminate information about child rights;
(f) To compile and analyse data on children;
(g) To promote the incorporation of child rights into the school

curriculum, teachers' training and training of personnel dealing with children.

The function has been performed keeping in mind the function of Commission for Protection of Child Rights Act, 2005 particularly Section 13(1) of the Commission for Protection of Child Rights Act, 2005 which stipulates the following functions:

(a) To examine and review the safeguards provided by or under any law for the time being in force for the Protection of Child Rights and recommend measures for their effective implementation;
(b) to present to the State Government annually and at such other interval, as the Commission may deem fit, the reports upon the working of those safeguards;
(c) to inquire into the cases of violation of Child Rights and to recommend the authorities concerned to take action;
(d) to examine all factors that inhibit the enjoyment of Rights of children affected by terrorism, communal violence, riots, natural disaster, domestic violence, HIV/AIDS, trafficking, maltreatment, torture and exploitation, pornography and prostitution and recommend appropriate remedial measures.
(e) to look into the matters related to children in need of special Care and Protection including children in distress, marginalized and disadvantaged children, children in Conflict with Law, children without family and children of prisoners and recommend appropriate remedial measures;
(f) to study treaties and other international instruments and undertake periodical review of existing policies, programmes and other activities on Child Rights and make recommendations for their effective implementation in the best interest of children;
(g) to undertake and promote research in the field of Child Rights;
(h) to spread Child Rights Literacy among various sections of the society and promote awareness of the safeguards available for protection of these rights through publications, media, seminars and other available means;

(i) to inspect or cause to be inspected any juvenile custodial home, or any other place of residence or institution meant for children, under the control of the Central Government or State Government or any other authority, detained or lodged for the purpose of treatment, reformation or protection and take up with these authorities for remedial action, if found necessary;

(j) To inquire into complaints and take *suo motu* notice of matters relating to:
   (i) Deprivation and violation of Child Rights;
   (ii) Non-implementation of laws providing for protection and development of children;
   (iii) Non-compliance of policy decision guidelines or instructions aimed at mitigating hardships to and ensuring welfare of the children and to provide relief to such children, or take up the issues arising out of such matters with appropriate authorities.

(k) Such other functions as it may consider necessary for the promotion of Child Rights and any other matter incidental to the above functions.

Section 13(2) states that the Commission shall not inquire into any matter which is pending before a State Commission or any other Commission duly constituted under any law for the time being in force.

In addition to this Act, there are also some Acts which aim to address the issues of human trafficking in India, such as, Prohibition of Child Marriage Act, 2006, Young Person (Harmful Publication) Act, 1956, Bonded Labour System (Abolition) Act, 1976, Indecent Representation of Women (Prohibition) Act, 1986, and the Transplantation Human Organs Act, 1994.

(iii) Committee for Combating Child Trafficking

The Government of Manipur has taken up various measures for combating child trafficking by constituting various high level committees. The Government has constituted a State Level Committee to Combat Child Trafficking headed by Chief Secretary. The Commissioner, Social Welfare, Government of Manipur shall be the Member Secretary of the committee and Director General of Police; Law Secretary; Director, Social Welfare; Director, Education(s); Director, Transport; Director, Health Services; Director, DIPR and NGOs working in the field of Children shall be members of the Committee.[12]

Table 4.4: State Level Committee to Combat Child Trafficking

Sl. No.	Remark	Designation
1.	Chief Secretary, Government of Manipur	Chairman
2.	Commissioner, Social Welfare, Government of Manipur	Member-Secretary
3.	Director General of Police, Manipur	Member
4.	Secretary (Law), Government of Manipur	Member
5.	Director, Social Welfare, Government of Manipur	Member
6.	Director of Education(s), Government of Manipur	Member
7.	Director, Transport Department, Government of Manipur	Member
8.	Director Health Services, Government of Manipur	Member
9.	Director (DIPR), Government of Manipur	Member
10.	NGOs working in the field of Children	Member

The Government of Manipur has also constituted a State Advisory Committee for Prevention and Combating Trafficking of Women and Children for Commercial Sexual Exploitation. The Chief Secretary and Director, Social Welfare, Government of Manipur shall be the Chairman and Member Secretary of the said committee which consists of six other members.[13]

Table 4.5: State Advisory Committee for Prevention and Combating Trafficking of Women and Children for Commercial Sexual Exploitation

Sl. No.	Remark	Designation
1.	Chief Secretary, Government of Manipur	Chairman
2.	Director General of Police, Government of Manipur	Member
3.	Principal Secretary (Labour), Government of Manipur	Member
4.	Commissioner (Social Welfare), Government of Manipur	Member
5.	Commissioner (Home), Government of Manipur	Member
6.	Secretary (Law), Government of Manipur	Member
7.	Director (Prosecution), Government of Manipur	Member
8.	Director, Social Welfare, Government of Manipur	Member

The Government of Manipur, with a view to checking the movement of children from this state to other states of India, has constituted a Dedicated Cell in the Department of Social Welfare Manipur. The Cell headed by the Director, Social Welfare, Government of Manipur aimed at establishing a system for interaction/interface of parent with the children living outside the state of Manipur and *vice versa* and addressing their grievances.[14]

Table 4.6: Dedicated Cell

Sl. No.	*Remark*	*Designation*
1.	Director, Social Welfare, Government of Manipur	Chairman
2.	Deputy Director (ICDS), Government of Manipur	Member
3.	Deputy Director (Social Welfare), Government of Manipur	Member
4.	Women Development Officer (Social Welfare), Government of Manipur	Member
5.	Child Welfare Officer (Social Welfare), Government of Manipur	Member
6.	Probation Officer (Social Welfare), Government of Manipur	Member
7.	State Programme Manager (ICPS)	Member

The Department of Social Welfare, Government of Manipur has issued a memorandum on the 5th April, 2010 notifying the constitution of District Level Anti-Trafficking Squad of the social welfare to tackle issues pertaining to human trafficking of women and children at the district level. The Anti-Trafficking Squad shall be headed by the DPO, ICDS, District Social Welfare Officer, CDPOs, ICDS and Supervisors, ICDS Project shall be members of the concerned districts and also shall be members of the committee.[15] The Department has also issued another office memorandum in consonance with the direction of the Supreme Court passed on the 1st Sept. 2010, in the case of the Exploitation of Children in Orphanage in the State of Tamil Nadu *Vs* Union of India [WP (C) No. 102 of 2007]. The Department, in compliance with the order of the Supreme Court, disallowed to send children who are below the age of 12 years or those who are in primary level outside the state of Manipur for perusing education.[16] However, despite having such state and district level bodies it is found that the state is not in a position to prevent human trafficking particularly women and child trafficking. The working of such Committees needs to be strengthened to combat child trafficking in the State of Manipur.

(f) Schemes Related to Human Trafficking *viz-a-viz* Ministry of Women and Child Development

(i) Integrated Child Protection Scheme

The Integrated Child Protection Scheme (ICPS) was launched in 2009, in partnership with the State Governments/UT Administrations, in order to strengthen prevention of child rights violation; enhanced infrastructure for protection services; provided financial support for implementation of the Juvenile Justice (Care and Protection of Children) Act, 2000; increased access to a wider range and better quality of protection services; increased investment in child protection and is continuously drawing focus on the right of all children to be safe. The Integrated Child Protection Scheme (ICPS) has significantly contributed to the realization of Government/State responsibility for creating a system that will efficiently and effectively protect children. Based on the cardinal principles of "protection of child rights" and "best interest of the child", ICPS is achieving its objectives to contribute to the improvements in the well-being of children in difficult circumstances, as well as to the reduction of vulnerabilities to situations and actions that lead to abuse, neglect, exploitation, abandonment and separation of children from their families.

The scheme aims at achieving the following objectives:

(a) To institutionalize essential services and strengthen structures for emergency outreach, institutional care, family and community based care, counselling and support services at the national, regional, state and district levels;
(b) To enhance capacities at all levels, of all functionaries including, administrators and service providers, members of allied systems including, local bodies, police, judiciary and other concerned departments of State Governments to undertake responsibilities under the ICPS;
(c) To create database and knowledge base for child protection services, including MIS and child tracking system in the country for effective implementation and monitoring of child protection services;
(d) Undertake research and documentation;

(e) To strengthen child protection at family and community level, create and promote preventive measures to protect children from situations of vulnerability, risk and abuse;

(f) To ensure appropriate inter-sectoral response at all levels, coordinate and network with all allied systems;

(g) To raise public awareness, educate public on child rights and protection on situation and vulnerabilities of children and families, on available child protection services, schemes and structures at all levels.

(ii) Childline

CHILDLINE is the country's first toll-free tele-helpline for street children in distress in the year 1996. It was launched by CHILDLINE India Foundation (CIF), Mumbai. The Objectives of CHILDLINE includes the following:

(a) To reach out to every child in need of care and protection by responding to emergencies on 1098.

(b) Awareness about CHILDLINE 1098 amongst every Indian child.

(c) To provide a platform of networking amongst organisations and to provide linkages to support systems that facilitates the rehabilitation of children in need of care and protection.

(d) To work together with the Allied Systems (Police, Health Care, Juvenile Justice, Transport, Legal, Education, Communication, Media, Political and the Community) to create child friendly systems.

(e) To advocate services for children that are inaccessible or non-existent.

(f) To create a body of NGOs and Government organisations working within the national framework and policy for children.

(g) To be a nodal child protection agency in the country, providing child protection services to children in need of care and protection.

(h) To contribute and work towards strengthening and participating in a global movement that addresses issues related to child protection and ensures that children's voices are heard.

(iii) The Ujjawala

Apart from initiating legislative measures, Government of India, Ministry of Women and Child Development formulated a Comprehensive Scheme for Prevention of Trafficking and Rescue, Rehabilitation and Reintegration of Victims of Trafficking for Commercial Sexual Exploitation. The *Ujjawala* scheme has five specific objectives for prevention, rescue, rehabilitation, reintegration and repatriation of victim of women and child trafficking in India. The objectives of the scheme may be reproduced as under:

(a) To prevent trafficking of women and children for commercial sexual exploitation through social mobilization and involvement of local communities, awareness generation programmes, generate public discourse through workshops/seminars and such events and any other innovative activity.
(b) To facilitate rescue of victims from the place of their exploitation and place them in safe custody.
(c) To provide rehabilitation services both immediate and long term to the victims by providing basic amenities/ needs such as shelter, food, clothing, medical treatment including counselling, legal aid and guidance and vocational training.
(d) To facilitate reintegration of the victims into the family and society at large.
(e) To facilitate repatriation of cross-border victims to their country of origin.

As per the scheme the followings are the targeted group:

(a) Women and children who are vulnerable to trafficking for commercial sexual exploitation.
(b) Women and children who are victims of trafficking for commercial sexual exploitation.

The implementing agencies of the *Ujjawala* schemes can be the SocialWelfare/Women and Child Welfare Department of State Government, Women's Development Corporations, Women's

Development Centres, Urban Local Bodies, reputed Public/Private Trust or Voluntary Organizations. The organization must have adequate experience in the field of trafficking, social defence, dealing with women and children in need of care and protection, children in conflict with law, etc.

(iv) Swadhar—A Scheme for Women in Difficult Circumstances

In order to prevent women from exploitation and to support their survival and rehabilitation, the scheme of Short Stay Home for women and girls was introduced as a social defence mechanism, by the then Department of Social Welfare in 1969. The scheme is meant to provide temporary accommodation, maintenance and rehabilitative services to women and girls rendered homeless due to family discord, crime, violence, mental stress, social ostracism or are being forced into prostitution and are in moral danger. Another scheme with the similar objectives namely Swadhar –A Scheme for Women in Difficult Circumstances was launched by the Department of Women and Child Development in 2001-02. The scheme works through the provisions of shelter, food, clothing, counselling, training, clinical and legal aid aims to rehabilitate such women in difficult circumstances. The scheme envisions a supportive institutional framework for women victims of difficult circumstances so that they could lead their life with dignity and conviction. It envisages that shelter, food, clothing, and health as well as economic and social security are assured for such women. It also envisions that the special needs of these women are properly taken care of and under no circumstances they should be left unattended or abandoned which could lead to their exploitation and desolation.

The Swadhar Greh is to set up short stay home in every district with capacity of 30 women with the following objectives:

(a) To cater to the primary need of shelter, food, clothing, medical treatment and care of the women in distress and who are without any social and economic support.
(b) To enable them to regain their emotional strength that gets hampered due to their encounter with unfortunate circumstances.
(c) To provide them with legal aid and guidance to enable

them to take steps for their readjustment in family/society.

(d) To rehabilitate them economically and emotionally.

(e) To act as a support system that understands and meets various requirements of women in distress.

(f) To enable them to start their life afresh with dignity and conviction.

The scheme shall cover women above 18 years of age of the following categories:

(a) Women who are deserted and are without any social and economic support;

(b) Women survivors of natural disasters who have been rendered homeless and are without any social and economic support;

(c) Women prisoners released from jail and are without family, social and economic support;

(d) Women victims of domestic violence, family tension or discord, who are made to leave their homes without any means of subsistence and have no special protection from exploitation and/or facing litigation on account of marital disputes; and

(e) Trafficked women/girls rescued or runaway from brothels or other places where they face exploitation and women affected by HIV/AIDS who do not have any social or economic support. However, such women/girls should first seek assistance under UJJAWALA Scheme in areas where it is in operation.

Women affected by domestic violence could stay up to one year. For other categories of women, the maximum period of stay could be up to 3 years. The older women above 55 years of age may be accommodated for maximum period of 5 years after which they will have to shift to old age homes or similar institutions. Swadhar Greh facilities could also be availed by the children accompanying women in the above categories. Girls up to the age of 18 years and boys up to the age of 8 years would be allowed to stay in the Swadhar Greh with their mothers. (Boys of more than 8 years of age need to be shifted to the Children Homes run under JJ Act/ICPS.)

Notes

1. Benjamin N. Cardozo, *The Nature of the Judicial Process*, Universal Law Publishing, Delhi, Eight Indian Reprint 2010, p. 83.
2. AIR 1990 SC 1412.
3. AIR 1997 SC 3021.
4. National Commission for Protection of Child Rights (No Date), *Concept Note: A Regional Consultation on Child Trafficking from and into 8 North Eastern States of India 2014-15.*
5. No. 24013/62/2012 – SC/ST–W
   Government of India, Ministry of Home Affairs, Centre State Division, Dated 25th June, 2013.
6. Section 30 of the JJ Act, 2015.
7. National Commission for Protection of Child Rights (No Date), *Concept Note: A Regional Consultation on Child Trafficking from and into 8 North Eastern States of India 2014-15.*
8. Ministry of Home Affairs, Government of India, 2015-2016, pp. 71-72.
9. Compiled by authors from the websites of Ministry of Home Affairs and Ministry of External Affairs, Government of India.
10. Sapam Dilipkumar, *Child Rights in Manipur*, Waba Publications, Imphal, 2016, p. 100.
11. Parliamentary institutions and Good Governance.
12. Order No. 9/26/2009-S (SW) pt. dt. 7/4/2010, Department of Social Welfare, Government of Manipur.
13. Order No. 2/11/(1A)/2009-H, dt. the 4th March, 2011, Department of Home, Government of Manipur.
14. Order No. 9/25/2009-S (SW) dt. the 15th October, 2011, Department of Social Welfare, Government of Manipur.
15. Order No. 9/14/2010-SW (JJA) dt. 5th April, 2010, Department of Social Welfare, Government of India.
16. Order No. 16/10/2010-S(SW) dt. the 2nd November, 2010, Department of Social Welfare, Government of Manipur.

5
Conclusion and Recommendations

1. The main cause of child trafficking in Manipur is mostly due to the need for quality school education and not merely because of poverty. The government school education system is not able to maintain quality, in spite of huge investment by the government (state and central). It is very unfortunate to observe that the infrastructure of government schools remain more or less the same since its inception and is considered obsolete. However, in the last few years, particularly in 2016, it is observed that, the search for employment opportunities is also manifested as one of the main causes of child trafficking in Manipur. This factor was also noticed in the earlier years but their number was insignificant. But, the two main factors have been significantly noticed simultaneously in the last few years.
2. The mode of recruitment for child trafficking is mostly through the local agents who, in almost all cases, are members of the community or from the same village where the victim resides. But, due to lack of factual information, it is not able to ascertain the direct involvement of these local agents. Lack of information is mostly due to the fact that the family and relatives of the victim are convinced in such a way that most of them do moved out of the state or their villages by themselves. In this process, the real or fake Christian missionaries play a major role as the traffickers know that their prospective target groups are believers of Christianity. So it makes them easy to convince and also secure their operations.

3. The route for trafficking seems to be multiplied with the increasing number of trafficking incidents. For instance, we have different routes to go to Guwahati from Imphal. But our concern is the change of direction. For instance, the main route for trafficking was towards Guwahati-Kolkata and finally to South Indian states particularly Tamil Nadu. But, we have noticed that the number of cases relating to trafficking of children in the name of providing quality education has been increased and distributed all over India. It is also found that the victims of inter-country trafficking was carried out by air through Imphal-Guwahati-Kolkota and then to Singapore. In addition to Guwahati direction, now we have noticed that the victims are being trafficked through the Imphal-Moreh in India and towards Myanmar and finally destined to Singapore. It does not mean that, this new route is the main route of inter-country trafficking. But, there is also a possibility of using multiple routes. The change of route may be because of its proximity to international border (approximately 3 hour from Imphal) and at the same time, the costs of travelling will considerably less. Besides, the conflict situation and corrupt practices prevailing in the state of Manipur might help them to easily evade the government machineries.
4. The government interventions that are specific to child trafficking seem to be taking backseat. For instance, the activities of the District Child Welfare Committees constituted under the JJ Act, 2015, which is the main statutory body to combat and rehabilitate the victim of child trafficking, remain ineffective because of various visible and invisible factors. For instance, it has been a practice of the state government that the allowances of the Chairpersons and members of Child Welfare Committees and other fund components have not been released in time. As stated in the memorandum submitted to the Shrimati Maneka Gandhi, Union Minister, Women and Child Development, by the joint representation of the CWCs of the State on 11 November, 2016, that there it is usually taking twelve to eighteen months to release the fund component of CWCs or even sometimes more. When

it is released, it is released in a piecemeal manner for only three to six months. Same is the case for the earlier members whose allowances have not been paid till now. Besides, there is no infrastructure for the CWCs, they operate from rented building and the office moves from place to place depending upon the chairperson of the CWCs. The fund meant for renting office and maintenance has not been paid regularly. This situation of ineffectiveness seems to have been exploited by the traffickers. For instance, there are two major reported incidents of trafficking in 2016, (i) 100 children were trafficked to illegal homes in Tamil Nadu and (ii) 100 girls were reported to have been trafficked to Singapore via Myanmar for employment. This came to light when the traffickers were arrested in the process of trafficking in the second attempt. The case is now taken up by Manipur Commission for Protection of Child Rights through the Ministry of External Affairs, Government of India.

5. The Committees constituted by the State Government such as State Level Committee to Combat Child Trafficking headed by Chief Secretary; State Advisory Committee for Prevention and Combating Trafficking of Women and Children for Commercial Sexual Exploitation headed by the Chief Secretary; and District Level Anti-Trafficking Squad headed by Director, Department of Social Welfare, Government of India seem to have limited activities. Their activities did not even find a space of their respective departmental annual reports.

Recommendations

1. As the main cause of child trafficking is search for quality school education, there is the urgent need to rejuvenate the school education system in Manipur. A time-bound 'Manipur School Education Commission' headed by an academician should be constituted with members drawn from various walks of life. The committee should be jointly monitored by the Manipur Commission for Protection of Child Rights and Directorate of Education (School), Government of Manipur.

2. As the CWCs of Manipur are in a pathetic condition, there is a need for seriously strengthening the CWCs by the government at the earliest. As a first step, they should clear the long pending dues and establish a permanent office with required support staff. Further, a study to examine the status of CWCs of Manipur, similar to that of the study undertaken by the National Commission for Protection of Child Rights should be conducted at the earliest.
3. As the government Committees including the high level committee remain invisible even in the respective departmental annual administrative reports, there is a need to restructure the committees, so as to create more space for members who can fully dedicate to the mandate of the committees. The involvement of government officials particularly the heads of department, who are already overloaded with their departmental activities should be minimised.
4. As the process to influence the victim families and relatives was mostly done at the village level, there is an urgent need to sensitise the village level government institutions and responsible villager officials including the women about the causes and consequences of child trafficking. The Manipur Commission for Protection of Child Rights should take the responsibility of the programme in consultation with NCPCR, Department of Social Welfare, Government of Manipur and its link departments or stakeholders.
5. The stakeholders such as Department of Social Welfare, Police Department, Directorate of Education (School), Health Department, Municipal or Panchayat Authorities, District Administration, in consultation with the Manipur Commission for Protection of Child Rights and NGOs working for the promotion and protection of child rights should converse their responsibilities in combating child trafficking in the state of Manipur. The Department of Social Welfare could be identified as the nodal department for making effective linkage among the stakeholders.
6. Considering the importance of the central security forces deployed in Manipur under the Ministry of Home and Ministry of Defence, their role is pivotal in combating child

trafficking as they are deployed in sensitive and border areas, where the state machinery presence is limited. Besides rescuing the victims, they can provide crucial information to the stakeholders as discussed above. For instance, there were reported cases of rescuing of child trafficking in the Indo-Myanmar region particularly Moreh by the central security forces. Thus, there is an urgent need to sensitise them particularly who are deployed in the border areas. However, for effective coordination, there is a need to set up a coordination committee for the state and central security forces in order to share information and exchange of ideas for combating child trafficking.

7. As we experienced that the lack of systematic documentation has weakened the data for child trafficking in Manipur, there is a need to develop an official format for documentation. This will help to document the cases in a continuous process irrespective of the capacity, commitment and creativity of the responsible person, which we feel is the practice in the state.
8. As the Government of Manipur is only implementing laws enacted by the Parliament and policies formulated by the Central Government to combat child trafficking, it is recommended to formulate and adopt a State Child Policy at the earliest. Further, in order to contextualise the policy, Manipur Commission for Protection of Child Rights should invite different stakeholders (State and non-State) of the state should be involved in formulating the policy. A review of the existing State Plan of Action for Children adopted by the Department of Social Welfare could be the beginning in formulating the policy.

Annexures

Annexure 1

Trafficking of Persons (Prevention, Protection and Rehabilitation) Bill 2016—DRAFT

A

BILL

to prevent trafficking of persons and to provide protection and rehabilitation to the victims of trafficking and to create a legal, economic, and social environment against trafficking of persons and for matters connected therewith or incidental thereto

WHEREAS, clause (1) of article 23 of Constitution of India prohibits trafficking in human beings and *begar* and other similar forms of forced labour, making a contravention of the same a punishable offence;

AND WHEREAS, article 21 of Constitution of India guarantees that no person shall be deprived of his life or personal liberty except according to the procedure established by law;

AND WHEREAS, the Government of India has ratified the United Nations Convention on Transnational Organised Crime and its three Optional Protocols, including the Protocol to Prevent, Suppress and Punish Trafficking in Persons, especially women and children;

AND WHEREAS, trafficking of persons needs to be prevented and the victims need care, protection and rehabilitation.

Be it enacted by Parliament in the Sixty-seventh Year of the Republic of India as follows:

Chapter I
Preliminary

1. Short title, extent, commencement and application—This Act may be called Trafficking of Persons (Prevention, Protection and Rehabilitation) Act, 2016.

(2) It extends to the whole of India, except the State of Jammu and Kashmir.

(3) It shall come into force on such date as the Central Government may, by notification in the Official Gazette, appoint.

2. Definitions—In this Act, unless the context otherwise requires, -

(a) "aftercare" means making provisions for support, financial or otherwise as prescribed by the appropriate Government, to a victim, who has left the Special Home and in the opinion of the District Anti-Trafficking Committee ready to reintegrate to join mainstream society;

(b) "appropriate Government" means the Central Government or a State Government, as the case may be;

(c) "child" means a person who has not completed eighteen years of age;

(d) "District Anti-Trafficking Committee" means a Committee established by the appropriate government under sub-section (1) of section 3;

(e) "Fund" means the Anti-Trafficking Fund created under section 29;

(f) "narcotic drugs" shall have the same meaning assigned to it in clause (xiv) of section 2 of Narcotic Drugs and Psychotropic Substances Act, 1985;

(g) "notification" means a notification published in the Official Gazette;

(h) "placement agency" shall mean a person or body of persons whether incorporated or not other than a Government agency, department or organisation engaged in the business of providing the service of employment to any person;

(i) "prescribed" means prescribed by rules made by the appropriate Government under this Act;

(j) "Protection Home" means a home established or maintained in every district or a group of districts, by the appropriate

Government directly, or through voluntary or non-governmental organisations, for the immediate care and protection of victims and for the purposes specified under section 8;

(k) "psychotropic substances" shall have the same meaning as assigned to it in clause (xxiii) of section 2 of Narcotic Drugs and Psychotropic Substances Act, 1985;

(l) "Special Home" means an institution, established or maintained, in every district or two or more districts by the appropriate Government, either directly or through a voluntary or non-Governmental organisation, and is registered as such for the purposes specified in section 9;

(m) "Special Court" means a Court of Session specified as a Special Court under Section 23;

(n) "Special Agency" means a Specialized Agency under section 7;

(o) "investigating officer" means an officer designated as such under section 28;

(p) "State Anti-trafficking Committee" means a Committee constituted by the appropriate Government under sub-section (1) of section 5;

(q) "victim" means a person or persons on whom trafficking of persons is caused or attempted by any other person or persons;

(r) "Welfare Officer" means a person in charge of the management of a Protection Home or Special Home and monitoring of individual care plans of all victims in such homes under this Act;

(s) words and expressions used but not defined in this Act and defined in the Juvenile Justice (Care and Protection of Children) Act, 2015 shall have the meanings respectively assigned to them in that Act.

CHAPTER II
DISTRICT ANTI-TRAFFICKING COMMITTEE

3. (1) The appropriate Government shall, by notification, constitute for every district, a District Anti-Trafficking Committee, for exercising the powers and performing such functions and duties in relation to prevention, rescue, protection, medical care,

psychological assistance, skill development, need based rehabilitation of victims as may be prescribed.

(2) The District Anti-Trafficking Committee shall consist of the following members, namely:

(i) the District Magistrate or District Collector- Chairperson;
(ii) two social workers out of which one shall be a woman to be nominated by the District Judge - Member;
(iii) one representative from the District Legal Services Authority nominated by the District Judge- Member;
(iv) District Officer of the Social Justice or Women and Child Development Department of the concerned States/UTs -Member Secretary.

(3) The District Anti- Trafficking Committee shall meet atleast once in three months.

(4) The District Anti- Trafficking Committee shall regulate its own procedure for conducting its meetings.

4. Procedure in relation to victims of trafficking of persons— (1) A victim, after rescue shall be produced before the Member Secretary of the District Anti-Trafficking Committee by:

(i) investigating officer or any police officer; or
(ii) any public servant; or
(iii) any social worker or public spirited citizen; or
(iv) by the victim himself, including if the victim is a child.

CHAPTER III
STATE ANTI-TRAFFICKING COMMITTEE

5. (1) The appropriate Government shall establish State Anti-Trafficking Committee to oversee the implementation of this Act and advise the State/UT Government and District Anti-Trafficking Committee on matters relating to prevention of trafficking, protection and rehabilitation of victims of trafficking in persons and to perform such other functions and duties as maybe prescribed.

(2) State Anti-Trafficking Committee constituted for a State/ UT, shall consist of the following members, namely:

(i) the Chief Secretary- Chairperson;
(ii) Secretary to the Department of the State dealing with

Women and Child-Member;

(iii) Secretary of the State Home Department - Member;

(iv) Secretary of the State Labour Department- Member;

(v) Secretary from State Health Department- Member;

(vi) Director General of Police of the concerned State- Member;

(vii) Secretary of the State Legal Services Authority - Member;

(viii) two social workers out of which one shall be a woman and to be nominated by the Chief Justice of the High Court - Member.

CHAPTER IV

6. Central Anti-Trafficking Advisory Board—(1) The Central Government shall constitute a Central Anti-Trafficking Advisory Board headed by the Secretary, Ministry of Women and Child Development and representatives from the concerned Ministries, State/UTs and members from civil society organisations as may be prescribed;

(2) Central Anti-Trafficking Advisory Board shall oversee the implementation of the Act and advise the appropriate Government on matters relating to prevention of trafficking, protection and rehabilitation of victims, in the manner as maybe prescribed.

CHAPTER V

7. Special Agency—The Central Government shall constitute a Special Agency for investigation of offences under the provisions of the Act.

CHAPTER VI
SUPPORT SERVICES

8. Protection Homes—(1) The appropriate Government shall maintain either directly or through voluntary organisations, protection homes selected and managed in the manner, as may be prescribed for the immediate care and protection of the victims.

(2) Protection Homes shall provide for shelter, food, clothing, counselling and medical care that is necessary for the rescued victims and such other services in the manner, as may be prescribed.

9. Special Homes—The appropriate Government shall maintain either directly or through voluntary organisations or use the existing shelter homes, as the case may be, one or more Special Homes in each district for the purpose of providing long-term institutional support for the rehabilitation of victims, in the manner as may be prescribed.

10. Registration of Homes—Notwithstanding anything contained in any other law for the time being in force, the Protection Homes and the Special Homes, shall be registered under this Act in such manner as may be prescribed by the appropriate Government.

CHAPTER VII
REHABILITATION AND SOCIAL INTEGRATION

11. (1) The appropriate Government shall frame schemes and programmes, in such manner as maybe prescribed, for the purpose of providing rehabilitation, support and after care services necessary for the social integration into mainstream society of the victims and to prevent re-trafficking.

(2) The State Government shall create specialised schemes for victims, especially for women engaged in prostitution or any other form of commercial sexual exploitation, to enable them to come forward and reintegrate into mainstream society, in a manner as may be prescribed.

CHAPTER VIII
REGISTRATION OF PLACEMENT AGENCIES

12. (1) Every placement agency, whether registered under any law for the time being in force or not, shall be registered for the purposes of this Act, within such time and manner as may be prescribed by the appropriate Government.

(2) The period of registration and the conditions for registration shall be in the manner as may be prescribed, by the appropriate Government.

(3) Notwithstanding anything contained in any other law for the time being in force, if any placement agency which violates any of the conditions of registration under sub-section (2) of section 12, the registration of such placement agency is liable to be

suspended, cancelled or revoked, as the case may be:

Provided that the placement agency shall be given an opportunity to be heard before any action is taken against it.

CHAPTER IX
OFFENCES AND PENALTIES

13. Any person in-charge of Protection Home or Special Home providing shelter to the victims contravenes any of the provisions of section 10, shall be punished with imprisonment which may extend to one year or with a fine not less than one lakh rupees, or with both.

14. Any person who contravenes the provisions of sub-section (1) of section 12 of this Act, shall be punishable with fine which may extend to one lakh rupees and any person who contravenes the provisions of sub-section (2) of section 12 shall be punishable with imprisonment for a term which may extend to 3 years or with fine which may extend to fifty thousand rupees, or with both.

15. Punishment for disclosure of identity—(1) No report, or any newspaper, or magazine, or audio-visual media, or any other form of communication regarding any investigation or judicial procedure shall disclose the name, address, or any other particulars which may lead to the identification of a victim, or witness of a crime of trafficking in persons under this Act, or any other law for the time being in force, nor shall the picture of any such victim be published.

(2) The publisher or owner of the media or studio or photographic facilities or any person in-charge of publication who contravenes the provision of sub-section (1) shall be punishable with imprisonment for a term which may extend to six months or with fine which may extend to one lakh rupees, or with both.

16. Using narcotic drugs, psychotropic or alcoholic substances for trafficking—Notwithstanding anything contained in any other law for the time being in force, whoever uses any narcotic drug or psychotropic substance, or alcohol, for the purpose of trafficking shall be punishable with imprisonment for a term which shall not be less than seven years, but which may extend to ten years, and shall also be liable to fine which shall not be less than one lakh rupees.

17. Use of chemical substance or hormones for the purpose

of exploitation—Notwithstanding anything contained in any other law for the time being in force, whoever administers any chemical substance or hormones to a trafficked woman or a girl or a child for the purpose of early sexual maturity and exploitation shall be punishable with imprisonment for a term which shall not be less than seven years, but which may extend to ten years, and shall also be liable to fine which shall not be less than one lakh rupees.

18. General Penalty—Whoever, violates any of the directions given by the appropriate Government under this Act shall be punishable with imprisonment for a term which may extend to three months or with fine which may extend to twenty thousand rupees, or with both.

19. Offence to be cognizable and non-bailable—(1) Notwithstanding anything contained in the Code of Criminal Procedure, 1973 (2 of 1974), -

(a) no person accused of an offence under sections 16 and 17 shall be released on bail or on his own bond unless—

(i) the Special Public Prosecutor has been given an opportunity to oppose the application for such release; and

(ii) where the Special Public Prosecutor opposes the application, the court is satisfied that there are reasonable grounds for believing that he is not guilty of such offence and that he is not likely to commit any offence while on bail.

(2) The limitations on granting of bail specified in clause (a) of sub-section (1) are in addition to the limitations under the Code of Criminal Procedure, 1973 (2 of 1974), or any other law for the time being in force on granting of bail.

CHAPTER X
CONFISCATION, FORFEITURE AND ATTACHMENT OF PROPERTY

20. (1) Where a person is in possession or ownership of any property, and is accused of having committed an offence under section 16 and 17 of this Act or offences under section 370-373 of Indian Penal Code, 1860 and it is likely that such property be concealed, transferred or dealt with in any manner which may result in frustrating any proceedings, the Special Court may confiscate such property.

(2) Where a person has been convicted of any offence punishable under an offence referred to in sub-section (1), the Special Court may, in addition to awarding any punishment, by order in writing, declare that any property, movable or immovable or both, belonging to the person, which has been used for the commission of that offence or accrue thereby, shall stand forfeited to Government.

(3) Where any person is accused of any offence referred to in sub-section (1), it shall be open to the Special Court trying him to pass an order that all or any of the properties, movable or immovable or both, belonging to him, shall, during the period of such trial, be attached, and where such trial ends in conviction, the property so attached shall be liable to forfeiture to the extent it is required for the purpose of realization of any fine imposed by the Special Court.

Notwithstanding, anything contained under section 20, any order passed by the Special Court for confiscation, attachment or forfeiture of the property, as the case may be, shall not prejudicially affect the claim of any third person who acquired any right, claim or interest in the property through lawful consideration with lawful object.

21. Burden of proof—The burden of proving that the property so attached and confiscated as per Section 20, is not acquired or used in the commission of the offence under this Act, which he is named as accused shall be on such person.

22. Application for attachment of property—(1) Where the appropriate Government has reason to believe that any person has committed (whether after the commencement of this Act or not) any offence under this Act, the State Government or, as the case may be, the Central Government may, whether or not any Court has taken cognizance of the offence, authorize the making of an application to the District Judge within the local limits of whose jurisdiction the said person ordinarily resides or carries on business, for the attachment, under this Act of the money or other property which the State Government or, as the case may be, the Central Government believes the said person to have procured by means of the alleged offence, or if such money or property cannot for any reason be attached, or other property of the said person of value as nearly as may be equivalent to that of the aforesaid money or other property.

(2) The provisions of Order XXVII of the First Schedule to the Code of Civil Procedure, 1908, shall apply to proceedings for an order of attachment under this Act as they apply to suits by the Government.

(3) An application under sub-section (1) shall be accompanied by one or more affidavit, stating the grounds on which the belief that the said person has committed any scheduled offence is founded, and the amount of money or value of other property believed to have been procured by means of the alleged offence and the application shall also furnish the following:

- (i) any information available as to the location for the time being of any such money or other property, and shall, if necessary, give particulars, including the estimated value, of other property of the said person;
- (ii) the names and addresses of any other persons believed to have or to be likely to claim, any interest or title in the property of the said person.

CHAPTER XI
SPECIAL COURTS AND POWERS OF SPECIAL COURTS

23. Special Court—Notwithstanding anything contained in the Code of Criminal Procedure, 1973 for the purposes of providing a speedy trial of offences involving and punishable under sections 370 to 373 of the Indian Penal Code, 1860 and the offences under this Act, the State Government shall in consultation with the Chief Justice of the High Court, by notification in the Official Gazette, specify for each district, a Court of Session to be a Special Court.

24. Presumption of certain offences—Where a person is prosecuted for committing or abetting or attempting to commit any offence under section 16 and 17 of this Act or offences under section 370-373 of Indian Penal Code, 1860, the Special Court shall presume that such person has committed the offence, unless the contrary is proved.

25. Application of Criminal Procedure Code, 1973 to proceedings before the Court—Save as otherwise provided in this Act, the provisions of the Code of Criminal Procedure, 1973 (including the provisions as to bail and bonds) shall apply to the proceedings before a Special Court and for the purposes of the said provisions, the Special Court shall be deemed to be a Court of Sessions and the person conducting a prosecution before a Special Court, shall be deemed to be a Special Public Prosecutor.

26. Special Public Prosecutors—(1) For every Special Court, the appropriate Government shall, by notification in the Official Gazette, specify a Special Public Prosecutor for the purpose of conducting case or cases falling under this Act and offences under sections 370 to 373 of the Indian Penal Code, 1860.

(2) Every person appointed under this section shall be deemed to be a Public Prosecutor within the meaning of clause (u) of Section 2 of the Code of Criminal Procedure, 1973 (2 of 1974).

(3) A person shall not be qualified to be appointed as Special Public Prosecutor under this section unless possess ten years active practice as an Advocate before a Court of Session having good record of prosecution.

27. Procedure for recovery of fines—(1) Where, on preliminary inquiry, a Special Court or a District Anti- Trafficking Committee, as the case maybe, finds that any amount is due to a victim, including backwages for the period of employment, or any other losses, it shall order for the recovery of the same as per the provisions of section 421 of the Code of Criminal Procedure.

(2) Notwithstanding anything contained in any other law applicable for the time being in force, where a person has been convicted of an offence of trafficking the Special Court may, in addition to the punishment prescribed under the relevant laws also order the accused to pay all backwages, or any other arrear or any other amount due to the victim, in addition to a fine which shall not be less than Rupees five lakhs for each victim engaged by such trafficker.

(3) Where an offender has been sentenced to pay a fine, the Special Court shall initiate action for the recovery of such fine as an arrear of land revenue as per the section 421 of the Code of Criminal Procedure.

CHAPTER XII
MISCELLANEOUS

28. Investigating Officer—The State Government shall designate a police officer of the rank of Gazetted Officer to be an Investigating Officer for investigating offences under this Act and under section 370 to 373 of the Indian Penal Code, 1860.

29. Anti-Trafficking Fund—(1) The appropriate Government, as the case maybe, shall create a fund for the effective implementation of this Act and also for the welfare and rehabilitation of the victims, as maybe prescribed.

(2) There shall be credited to the fund such voluntary donations, contributions or subscriptions as may be made by any individual or organisation.

(3) The fund created under sub-section (1) shall be administered by the appropriate Government in such manner and for such purposes as may be prescribed by that Government.

30. Procedure for Mandatory reporting—Any police officer or a public servant, or any officer or employee of Protection home or Special home, who finds or takes charge of, or who is handed over the custody or care of a victim shall within twenty four hours, give information to the nearest police station, or a District Anti-Trafficking Committee or in the case of a child victim, to a Child Welfare Committee, or a child care institution registered under the provisions of the Juvenile Justice (Care and Protection) Act, 2015.

31. Repatriation to another state—A victim, on an order of the District Anti-Trafficking Committee or the Special Court may be repatriated to the home State or to another State for increased protection:

Provided the District Anti-Trafficking Committee of the recipient district may take over the rehabilitation of the victim in such manner as may be prescribed by the appropriate Government.

32. Repatriation to another Country—Where a victim from foreign country has been rescued and the State Anti-Trafficking Committee is of the opinion that the victim needs to be repatriated to the country of origin, it may be dealt with the matter under any law for the time being in force.

33. Appeal—(1) Notwithstanding anything contained in the Criminal Procedure Code, an appeal shall lie from any judgment, sentence or order, not being an interlocutory order, of a Special Court under sections 16 and 17 of this Act and sections 370-373 of the Indian Penal Code, 1860 to the High Court both on facts and on law.

(2) Every appeal under sub-section (1) shall be heard by a Division Bench of the High Court and shall, as far as possible, be

disposed of within a period of three months from the date of admission of the appeal.

(3) Except as aforesaid, no appeal or revision shall lie to any court from any judgment, sentence or order including an interlocutory order of a Special Court.

(4) Notwithstanding anything contained in sub-section (3) of section 378 of the Code, an appeal shall lie to the High Court against an order of the Special Court granting or refusing bail.

(5) Every appeal under this section shall be preferred within a period of thirty days from the date of the judgment, sentence or order appealed from:

Provided that the High Court may entertain an appeal after the expiry of the said period of thirty days if it is satisfied that the appellant had sufficient cause for not preferring the appeal within the period of thirty days:

Provided further that no appeal shall be entertained after the expiry of period of ninety days.

34. Protection of Action Taken in Good Faith—No suit, prosecution or other legal proceeding shall lie against the Central Government, or the State Government or any person acting under the directions of the Central Government or State Government, as the case may be, in respect of anything which is done in good faith or intended to be done in pursuance of this Act or of any rules or regulations made thereunder.

35. Power of Central Government to make Rules—The Central Government may, by notification in the Official Gazette, make rules for carrying out the provisions of this Act on the subject specified under this Act:

Provided that the Central Government may, frame model rules in respect of all or any of the matters with respect to which the State Government is required to make rules and where any such model rules have been framed in respect of any such matter, they shall apply to the State *mutatis mutandis* until the rules in respect of that matter are made by the State Government and while making any such rules, they conform to such model rules.

36. Power of the State Government to make rules—(1) The State Government may, by notification in the Official Gazette, make rules for carrying out the provisions of this Act.

(2) Every rule made under this Act shall be laid, as soon as may be after it is made, before each House of the State Legislature.

37. Power to give directions—The appropriate Government may give such directions as it may deem fit to any individual, person or body of persons or organisation, whether incorporated or not, in respect of any matter under this Act.

38. Laying of Rules—Every rule made by the Central Government under this Act shall be laid, as soon as may be after it is made, before each House of Parliament, while it is in session, for a total period of thirty days which may be comprised in one session or in two or more successive sessions, and if, before the expiry of the session immediately following the session or the successive sessions aforesaid, both Houses agree in making any modification in the rule or both Houses agree that the rule should not be made, the rule shall thereafter have effect only in such modified form or be of no effect, as the case may be; so, however, that any such modification or annulment shall be without prejudice to the validity of anything previously done under that rule.

39. Power to Remove Difficulty—If any difficulty arises in giving effect to the provisions of this Act, the Central Government may, by order, not inconsistent with the provisions of this Act, remove the difficulty:

Provided, that no such order shall be made after the expiry of the period of two years from the commencement of this Act.

40. Section 360 of the Code and Probation of Offenders Act, 1958 not to apply to persons committing an offence under this Act

The provisions of section 360 of the Code of Criminal Procedure, 1973 (2 of 1974) and the provisions of Offenders Act, 1958 (20 of 1958) shall not apply to any person above the age of eighteen years who is found guilty of having committed an offence under this Act.

41. Act to override other laws—Save as otherwise provided in this Act, the provisions of this Act or any rule made thereunder or any order made under any such rule shall, have effect notwithstanding anything inconsistent therewith contained in any other law for the time being in force or in any instrument having the force of law.

Annexure 2

SAARC Convention on Preventing and Combating Trafficking in Women and Children for Prostitution

THE MEMBER STATES OF THE SOUTH ASIAN ASSOCIATION FOR REGIONAL COOPERATION (SAARC), PARTIES TO THE PRESENT CONVENTION

EMPHASISING that the evil of trafficking in women and children for the purpose of prostitution is incompatible with the dignity and honour of human beings and is a violation of basic human rights;

RECALLING the decision of the Ninth SAARC Summit (May, 1997) that the feasibility of a regional Convention to combat the grave crime of trafficking in women and children for prostitution should be explored;

RECALLING ALSO the relevant international legal instruments relating to prevention of trafficking in women and children, including the Convention for the Suppression of Trafficking in Persons and of the Exploitation of Prostitution of Others, 1949; Convention on the Elimination of All Forms of Discrimination against Women, 1979; International Covenant on Civil and Political Rights, 1966; and the Convention on the Rights of the Child, 1989;

GIVING due regard to the implementation of the recommendations of the various pertinent International Bodies and Conferences including the Fourth World Conference on Women at Beijing (1995);

NOTING with concern the increasing exploitation by traffickers of women and children from SAARC countries and their increasing use of these countries as sending, receiving and transit points;

RECOGNISING in this regard the importance of establishing effective regional cooperation for preventing trafficking for prostitution and for investigation, detection, interdiction, prosecution and punishment of those responsible for such trafficking;

EMPHASISING **the need to strengthen cooperation in providing assistance, rehabilitation and repatriation to victims of trafficking for prostitution;**

HAVE AGREED **as follows:**

ARTICLE I
DEFINITIONS

For the purpose of this Convention:

(1) "Child" means a person who has not attained the age of 18 years;
(2) "Prostitution" means the sexual exploitation or abuse of persons for commercial purposes;
(3) "Trafficking" means the moving, selling or buying of women and children for prostitution within and outside a country for monetary or other considerations with or without the consent of the person subjected to trafficking;
(4) "Traffickers" means persons, agencies or institutions engaged in any form of trafficking;
(5) "Persons subjected to trafficking" means women and children victimised or forced into prostitution by the traffickers by deception, threat, coercion, kidnapping, sale, fraudulent marriage, child marriage, or any other unlawful means;
(6) "Protective home" means a home established or recognised by a Government of a Member State for the reception, care, treatment and rehabilitation of rescued or arrested persons subjected to trafficking.
(7) "Repatriation" means return to the country of origin of the person subjected to trafficking across international frontiers.

ARTICLE II
SCOPE OF THE CONVENTION

The purpose of this Convention is to promote cooperation amongst Member States so that they may effectively deal with the various aspects of prevention, interdiction and suppression of trafficking in women and children; the repatriation and rehabilitation of victims of trafficking and prevent the use of women and children in international prostitution networks, particularly where the countries of the SAARC region are the countries of origin, transit and destination.

ARTICLE III
OFFENCES

1. The State Parties to the Convention shall take effective measures to ensure that trafficking in any form is an offence under their respective criminal law and shall make such an offence punishable by appropriate penalties which take into account its grave nature.
2. The State Parties to the Convention, in their respective territories, shall provide for punishment of any person who keeps, maintains or manages or knowingly finances or takes part in the financing of a place used for the purpose of trafficking and knowingly lets or rents a building or other place or any part thereof for the purpose of trafficking.
3. Any attempt or abetment to commit any crime mentioned in paras 1 and 2 above or their financing shall also be punishable.

ARTICLE IV
AGGRAVATING CIRCUMSTANCES

1. The State Parties to the Convention shall ensure that their courts having jurisdiction over the offences committed under this Convention, can take into account factual circumstances which make the commission of such offences particularly grave, viz:
   (a) the involvement in the offences of an organised criminal group to which the offender belongs;
   (b) the involvement of the offender in other international organised criminal activities;
   (c) the use of violence or arms by the offender;
   (d) the fact that the offender holds a public office and that the offence is committed in misuse of that office;
   (e) the victimisation or trafficking of children;
   (f) the fact that the offence is committed in a custodial institution or in an educational institution or social facility or in their immediate vicinity or in other places

to which children and students visit for educational, sports, social and cultural activities;

(g) previous conviction, particularly for similar offences, whether in a Member State or any other country.

ARTICLE V
JUDICIAL PROCEEDINGS

In trying offences under this Convention, judicial authorities in Member States shall ensure that the confidentiality of the child and women victims is maintained and that they are provided appropriate counselling and legal assistance.

ARTICLE VI
MUTUAL LEGAL ASSISTANCE

1. The State Parties to the Convention shall grant to each other the widest measure of mutual legal assistance in respect of investigations, inquiries, trials or other proceedings in the requesting State in respect of offences under this Convention. Such assistance shall include:
   (a) taking of evidence and obtaining of statements of persons;
   (b) provision of information, documents and other records including criminal and judicial records;
   (c) location of persons and objects including their identification;
   (d) search and seizures;
   (e) delivery of property including lending of exhibits;
   (f) making detained persons and others available to give evidence or assist investigations;
   (g) service of documents including documents seeking attendance of persons; and
   (h) any other assistance consistent with the objectives of this Convention.
2. Requests for assistance shall be executed promptly in accordance with their national laws and in the manner requested by the Requesting State. In the event that the Requested State is not able to comply in whole or in part with a request for assistance or decides to postpone execution it shall promptly inform the Requesting State

and shall give reasons for the same.

ARTICLE VII
EXTRADITION OR PROSECUTION

1. The offences referred to in the present Convention shall be regarded as extraditable offences in any extradition treaty which has been or may hereinafter be concluded, between any of the Parties to the Convention.
2. If a State Party which makes extradition conditional on the existence of a treaty, receives a request for extradition from another State Party with which it has no extradition treaty, the Requested State shall, if so permitted by its laws, consider this Convention as the basis for extradition in respect of the offences set forth in Article III.
3. Extradition shall be granted in accordance with the laws of the State to which the request is made.
4. The State Party in whose territory the alleged offender is present shall, if it does not extradite him or her, submit, without exception whatsoever and without undue delay, the case to its competent authorities for the purpose of prosecution in accordance with the laws of that State.
5. In States where extradition of their nationals is not permitted under their law, nationals who have committed offences under the present Convention shall be prosecuted and punished by their courts.

ARTICLE VIII
MEASURES TO PREVENT AND INTERDICT TRAFFICKING IN WOMEN AND CHILDREN

1. The State Parties to the Convention shall provide sufficient means, training and assistance to their respective authorities to enable them to effectively conduct inquiries, investigations and prosecution of offences under this Convention.
2. The State Parties to the Convention shall sensitize their law enforcement agencies and the judiciary in respect of the offences under this Convention and other related factors that encourage trafficking in women and children.

3. The State Parties to the Convention shall establish a Regional Task Force consisting of officials of the Member States to facilitate implementation of the provisions of this Convention and to undertake periodic reviews.
4. The State Parties to the Convention may also, by mutual agreement, set up bilateral mechanisms to effectively implement the provisions of the Convention, including appropriate mechanisms for cooperation to interdict trafficking in women and children for prostitution.
5. The State Parties to the Convention shall exchange, on a regular basis, information in respect of agencies, institutions and individuals who are involved in trafficking in the region and also identify methods and routes used by the traffickers through land, water or air. The information so furnished shall include information of the offenders, their fingerprints, photographs, methods of operation, police records and records of conviction.
6. The State Parties to the Convention may consider taking necessary measures for the supervision of employment agencies in order to prevent trafficking in women and children under the guise of recruitment.
7. The State Parties to the Convention shall endeavour to focus preventive and development efforts on areas which are known to be source areas for trafficking.
8. The State Parties to the Convention shall promote awareness, *interalia,* through the use of the media, of the problem of trafficking in women and children and its underlying causes including the projection of negative images of women.

ARTICLE IX
CARE, TREATMENT, REHABILITATION AND REPATRIATION OF THE VICTIMS

1. The State Parties to the Convention shall work out modalities for repatriation of the victims to the country of origin.
2. Pending the completion of arrangements for the repatriation of victims of cross-border trafficking, the State Parties to the Convention shall make suitable provisions

for their care and maintenance. The provision of legal advice and health care facilities shall also be made available to such victims.

3. The State Parties to the Convention shall establish protective homes or shelters for rehabilitation of victims of trafficking. Suitable provisions shall also be made for granting legal advice, counselling, job training and health care facilities for the victims.
4. The State Parties to the Convention may also authorise the recognised non-governmental organisations to establish such protective homes or shelters for providing suitable care and maintenance for the victims of trafficking.
5. The State Parties to the Convention shall encourage recognised non-governmental organisations in efforts aimed at prevention, intervention and rehabilitation, including through the establishment of such protective homes or shelters for providing suitable care and maintenance for the victims of trafficking.

ARTICLE X
IMPLEMENTATION

The State Parties to the Convention shall adopt, in accordance with their respective Constitutions, the legislative and other measures necessary to ensure the implementation of the Convention.

ARTICLE XI
HIGHER MEASURES

The measures provided for in the Convention are without prejudice to higher measures of enforcement and protection accorded by relevant national laws and international agreements.

ARTICLE XII
SIGNATURE AND RATIFICATION

The Convention shall be open for signature by the Member States of SAARC at the Eleventh SAARC Summit at Kathmandu and thereafter, at the SAARC Secretariat at Kathmandu. It shall be subject to ratification. The Instruments of Ratification shall be deposited with the Secretary-General.

ARTICLE XIII
ENTRY INTO FORCE

This Convention shall enter into force on the fifteenth day following the day of the deposit of the seventh Instrument of Ratification with the Secretary-General.

ARTICLE XIV
DEPOSITORY

The Secretary-General shall be the depository of this Convention and shall notify the Member States of signatures to this Convention and all deposits of Instruments of Ratification. The Secretary-General shall transmit certified copies of such instruments to each Member State. The Secretary-General shall also inform Member States of the date on which this Convention will have entered into force in accordance with Article XIII.

IN WITNESS WHEREOF the undersigned, being duly authorised thereto by their respective Governments, have signed this Convention.

DONE at Kathmandu on this Fifth Day of January Two Thousand and Two, in nine originals, in the English Language, all texts being equally authentic.

M. MORSHED KHAN
Minister for Foreign Affairs
People's Republic of Bangladesh

JIGMI Y. THINLEY
Minister of Foreign Affairs
Kingdom of Bhutan

JASWANT SINGH
Minister of External Affairs
Republic of India

FATHULLA JAMEEL
Minister of Foreign Affairs
Republic of Maldives

RAM SHARAN MAHAT
Minister of Finance and Leader
of the Delegation of Nepal
Kingdom of Nepal

ABDUL SATTAR
Minister of Foreign Affairs
Islamic Republic of Pakistan

TYRONNE FERNANDO
Minister of Foreign Affairs
Democratic Socialist Republic of Sri Lanka

Annexure 3

Protocol to Prevent, Suppress and Punish Trafficking in Persons, Especially Women and Children, supplementing the United Nations Convention against Transnational Organized Crime

PREAMBLE

The States Parties to this Protocol,

Declaring that effective action to prevent and combat trafficking in persons, especially women and children, requires a comprehensive international approach in the countries of origin, transit and destination that includes measures to prevent such trafficking, to punish the traffickers and to protect the victims of such trafficking, including by protecting their internationally recognized human rights,

Taking into account the fact that, despite the existence of a variety of international instruments containing rules and practical measures to combat the exploitation of persons, especially women and children, there is no universal instrument that addresses all aspects of trafficking in persons,

Concerned that, in the absence of such an instrument, persons who are vulnerable to trafficking will not be sufficiently protected,

Recalling General Assembly resolution 53/111 of 9 December, 1998, in which the Assembly decided to establish an open-ended intergovernmental *ad hoc* committee for the purpose of elaborating a comprehensive international convention against transnational organized crime and of discussing the elaboration of, *inter alia,* an international instrument addressing trafficking in women and children,

Convinced that supplementing the United Nations Convention against Transnational Organized Crime with an international instrument for the prevention, suppression and punishment of trafficking in persons, especially women and children, will be useful in preventing and combating that crime,

Have agreed as follows:

I
GENERAL PROVISIONS

Article 1. Relation with the United Nations Convention against Transnational Organized Crime

1. This Protocol supplements the United Nations Convention against Transnational Organized Crime. It shall be interpreted together with the Convention.
2. The provisions of the Convention shall apply, *mutatis mutandis*, to this Protocol unless otherwise provided herein.
3. The offences established in accordance with article 5 of this Protocol shall be regarded as offences established in accordance with the Convention.

Article 2. Statement of purpose

The purposes of this Protocol are:

(a) To prevent and combat trafficking in persons, paying particular attention to women and children;
(b) To protect and assist the victims of such trafficking, with full respect for their human rights; and
(c) To promote cooperation among States Parties in order to meet those objectives.

Article 3. Use of terms

For the purposes of this Protocol:

(a) "Trafficking in persons" shall mean the recruitment, transportation, transfer, harbouring or receipt of persons, by means of the threat or use of force or other forms of coercion, of abduction, of fraud, of deception, of the abuse of power or of a position of vulnerability or of the giving or receiving of payments or benefits to achieve the consent of a person having control over another person, for the purpose of exploitation. Exploitation shall include, at a minimum, the exploitation of the prostitution of others or other forms of sexual exploitation, forced labour or services, slavery or practices similar to slavery, servitude or the removal of organs;

(b) The consent of a victim of trafficking in persons to the intended exploitation set forth in subparagraph *(a)* of this article shall be irrelevant where any of the means set forth in subparagraph *(a)* have been used;

(c) The recruitment, transportation, transfer, harbouring or receipt of a child for the purpose of exploitation shall be considered "trafficking in persons" even if this does not involve any of the means set forth in subparagraph *(a)* of this article;

(d) "Child" shall mean any person under eighteen years of age.

Article 4. Scope of application

This Protocol shall apply, except as otherwise stated herein, to the prevention, investigation and prosecution of the offences established in accordance with article 5 of this Protocol, where those offences are transnational in nature and involve an organized criminal group, as well as to the protection of victims of such offences.

Article 5. Criminalization

1. Each State Party shall adopt such legislative and other measures as may be necessary to establish as criminal offences the conduct set forth in article 3 of this Protocol, when committed intentionally.

2. Each State Party shall also adopt such legislative and other measures as may be necessary to establish as criminal offences:

(a) Subject to the basic concepts of its legal system, attempting to commit an offence established in accordance with paragraph 1 of this article;

(b) Participating as an accomplice in an offence established in accordance with paragraph 1 of this article; and

(c) Organizing or directing other persons to commit an offence established in accordance with paragraph 1 of this article.

II
PROTECTION OF VICTIMS OF TRAFFICKING IN PERSONS

Article 6. Assistance to and protection of victims of trafficking in persons

1. In appropriate cases and to the extent possible under its domestic law, each State Party shall protect the privacy and identity of victims of trafficking in persons, including, *inter alia*, by making legal proceedings relating to such trafficking confidential.

2. Each State Party shall ensure that its domestic legal or administrative system contains measures that provide to victims of trafficking in persons, in appropriate cases:

(a) Information on relevant court and administrative proceedings;

(b) Assistance to enable their views and concerns to be presented and considered at appropriate stages of criminal proceedings against offenders, in a manner not prejudicial to the rights of the defence.

3. Each State Party shall consider implementing measures to provide for the physical, psychological and social recovery of victims of trafficking in persons, including, in appropriate cases, in cooperation with non-governmental organizations, other relevant organizations and other elements of civil society, and, in particular, the provision of:

(a) Appropriate housing;

(b) Counselling and information, in particular as regards their legal rights, in a language that the victims of trafficking in persons can understand;

(c) Medical, psychological and material assistance; and

(d) Employment, educational and training opportunities.

4. Each State Party shall take into account, in applying the provisions of this article, the age, gender and special needs of victims of trafficking in persons, in particular the special needs of children, including appropriate housing, education and care.

5. Each State Party shall endeavour to provide for the physical safety of victims of trafficking in persons while they are within its territory.

6. Each State Party shall ensure that its domestic legal system contains measures that offer victims of trafficking in persons the possibility of obtaining compensation for damage suffered.

Article 7. Status of victims of trafficking in persons in receiving States

1. In addition to taking measures pursuant to article 6 of this Protocol, each State Party shall consider adopting legislative or other appropriate measures that permit victims of trafficking in persons to remain in its territory, temporarily or permanently, in appropriate cases.

2. In implementing the provision contained in paragraph 1 of this article, each State Party shall give appropriate consideration to humanitarian and compassionate factors.

Article 8. Repatriation of victims of trafficking in persons

1. The State Party of which a victim of trafficking in persons is a national or in which the person had the right of permanent residence at the time of entry into the territory of the receiving State Party shall facilitate and accept, with due regard for the safety of that person, the return of that person without undue or unreasonable delay.

2. When a State Party returns a victim of trafficking in persons to a State Party of which that person is a national or in which he or she had, at the time of entry into the territory of the receiving State Party, the right of permanent residence, such return shall be with due regard for the safety of that person and for the status of any legal proceedings related to the fact that the person is a victim of trafficking and shall preferably be voluntary.

3. At the request of a receiving State Party, a requested State Party shall, without undue or unreasonable delay, verify whether a person who is a victim of trafficking in persons is its national or had the right of permanent residence in its territory at the time of entry into the territory of the receiving State Party.

4. In order to facilitate the return of a victim of trafficking in

persons who is without proper documentation, the State Party of which that person is a national or in which he or she had the right of permanent residence at the time of entry into the territory of the receiving State Party shall agree to issue, at the request of the receiving State Party, such travel documents or other authorization as may be necessary to enable the person to travel to and re-enter its territory.

5. This article shall be without prejudice to any right afforded to victims of trafficking in persons by any domestic law of the receiving State Party.

6. This article shall be without prejudice to any applicable bilateral or multilateral agreement or arrangement that governs, in whole or in part, the return of victims of trafficking in persons.

III
PREVENTION, COOPERATION AND OTHER MEASURES

Article 9. Prevention of trafficking in persons

1. States Parties shall establish comprehensive policies, programmes and other measures:

   (a) To prevent and combat trafficking in persons; and

   (b) To protect victims of trafficking in persons, especially women and children, from revictimization.

2. States Parties shall endeavour to undertake measures such as research, information and mass media campaigns and social and economic initiatives to prevent and combat trafficking in persons.

3. Policies, programmes and other measures established in accordance with this article shall, as appropriate, include cooperation with non-governmental organizations, other relevant organizations and other elements of civil society.

4. States Parties shall take or strengthen measures, including through bilateral or multilateral cooperation, to alleviate the factors that make persons, especially women and children, vulnerable to trafficking, such as poverty, underdevelopment and lack of equal opportunity.

5. States Parties shall adopt or strengthen legislative or other measures, such as educational, social or cultural measures, including through bilateral and multilateral cooperation, to

discourage the demand that fosters all forms of exploitation of persons, especially women and children, that leads to trafficking.

Article 10. Information exchange and training

1. Law enforcement, immigration or other relevant authorities of States Parties shall, as appropriate, cooperate with one another by exchanging information, in accordance with their domestic law, to enable them to determine:

(a) Whether individuals crossing or attempting to cross an international border with travel documents belonging to other persons or without travel documents are perpetrators or victims of trafficking in persons;

(b) The types of travel document that individuals have used or attempted to use to cross an international border for the purpose of trafficking in persons; and

(c) The means and methods used by organized criminal groups for the purpose of trafficking in persons, including the recruitment and transportation of victims, routes and links between and among individuals and groups engaged in such trafficking, and possible measures for detecting them.

2. States Parties shall provide or strengthen training for law enforcement, immigration and other relevant officials in the prevention of trafficking in persons. The training should focus on methods used in preventing such trafficking, prosecuting the traffickers and protecting the rights of the victims, including protecting the victims from the traffickers. The training should also take into account the need to consider human rights and child- and gender-sensitive issues and it should encourage cooperation with non-governmental organizations, other relevant organizations and other elements of civil society.

3. A State Party that receives information shall comply with any request by the State Party that transmitted the information that places restrictions on its use.

Article 11. Border measures

1. Without prejudice to international commitments in relation to the free movement of people, States Parties shall strengthen, to

the extent possible, such border controls as may be necessary to prevent and detect trafficking in persons.

2. Each State Party shall adopt legislative or other appropriate measures to prevent, to the extent possible, means of transport operated by commercial carriers from being used in the commission of offences established in accordance with article 5 of this Protocol.

3. Where appropriate, and without prejudice to applicable international conventions, such measures shall include establishing the obligation of commercial carriers, including any transportation company or the owner or operator of any means of transport, to ascertain that all passengers are in possession of the travel documents required for entry into the receiving State.

4. Each State Party shall take the necessary measures, in accordance with its domestic law, to provide for sanctions in cases of violation of the obligation set forth in paragraph 3 of this article.

5. Each State Party shall consider taking measures that permit, in accordance with its domestic law, the denial of entry or revocation of visas of persons implicated in the commission of offences established in accordance with this Protocol.

6. Without prejudice to article 27 of the Convention, States Parties shall consider strengthening cooperation among border control agencies by, *inter alia*, establishing and maintaining direct channels of communication.

Article 12. Security and control of documents

Each State Party shall take such measures as may be necessary, within available means:

(a) To ensure that travel or identity documents issued by it are of such quality that they cannot easily be misused and cannot readily be falsified or unlawfully altered, replicated or issued; and

(b) To ensure the integrity and security of travel or identity documents issued by or on behalf of the State Party and to prevent their unlawful creation, issuance and use.

Article 13. Legitimacy and validity of documents

At the request of another State Party, a State Party shall, in accordance with its domestic law, verify within a reasonable time the legitimacy and validity of travel or identity documents issued or purported to have been issued in its name and suspected of being used for trafficking in persons.

IV
FINAL PROVISIONS

Article 14. Saving clause

1. Nothing in this Protocol shall affect the rights, obligations and responsibilities of States and individuals under international law, including international humanitarian law and international human rights law and, in particular, where applicable, the 1951 Convention[1] and the 1967 Protocol[2] relating to the Status of Refugees and the principle of non-refoulement as contained therein.

2. The measures set forth in this Protocol shall be interpreted and applied in a way that is not discriminatory to persons on the ground that they are victims of trafficking in persons. The interpretation and application of those measures shall be consistent with internationally recognized principles of non-discrimination.

Article 15. Settlement of disputes

1. States Parties shall endeavour to settle disputes concerning the interpretation or application of this Protocol through negotiation.

2. Any dispute between two or more States Parties concerning the interpretation or application of this Protocol that cannot be settled through negotiation within a reasonable time shall, at the request of one of those States Parties, be submitted to arbitration. If, six months after the date of the request for arbitration, those States Parties are unable to agree on the organization of the arbitration, any one of those States Parties may refer the dispute to the International Court of Justice by request in accordance with the Statute of the Court.

3. Each State Party may, at the time of signature, ratification, acceptance or approval of or accession to this Protocol, declare that it does not consider itself bound by paragraph 2 of this article.

The other States Parties shall not be bound by paragraph 2 of this article with respect to any State Party that has made such a reservation.

4. Any State Party that has made a reservation in accordance with paragraph 3 of this article may at any time withdraw that reservation by notification to the Secretary-General of the United Nations.

Article 16. Signature, ratification, acceptance, approval and accession

1. This Protocol shall be open to all States for signature from 12 to 15 December 2000 in Palermo, Italy, and thereafter at United Nations Headquarters in New York until 12 December 2002.

2. This Protocol shall also be open for signature by regional economic integration organizations provided that at least one member State of such organization has signed this Protocol in accordance with paragraph 1 of this article.

3. This Protocol is subject to ratification, acceptance or approval. Instruments of ratification, acceptance or approval shall be deposited with the Secretary-General of the United Nations. A regional economic integration organization may deposit its instrument of ratification, acceptance or approval if at least one of its member States has done likewise. In that instrument of ratification, acceptance or approval, such organization shall declare the extent of its competence with respect to the matters governed by this Protocol. Such organization shall also inform the depositary of any relevant modification in the extent of its competence.

4. This Protocol is open for accession by any State or any regional economic integration organization of which at least one member State is a Party to this Protocol. Instruments of accession shall be deposited with the Secretary-General of the United Nations. At the time of its accession, a regional economic integration organization shall declare the extent of its competence with respect to matters governed by this Protocol. Such organization shall also inform the depositary of any relevant modification in the extent of its competence.

Article 17. Entry into force

1. This Protocol shall enter into force on the ninetieth day after the date of deposit of the fortieth instrument of ratification, acceptance, approval or accession, except that it shall not enter into force before the entry into force of the Convention. For the purpose of this paragraph, any instrument deposited by a regional economic integration organization shall not be counted as additional to those deposited by member States of such organization.

2. For each State or regional economic integration organization ratifying, accepting, approving or acceding to this Protocol after the deposit of the fortieth instrument of such action, this Protocol shall enter into force on the thirtieth day after the date of deposit by such State or organization of the relevant instrument or on the date this Protocol enters into force pursuant to paragraph 1 of this article, whichever is the later.

Article 18. Amendment

1. After the expiry of five years from the entry into force of this Protocol, a State Party to the Protocol may propose an amendment and file it with the Secretary-General of the United Nations, who shall thereupon communicate the proposed amendment to the States Parties and to the Conference of the Parties to the Convention for the purpose of considering and deciding on the proposal. The States Parties to this Protocol meeting at the Conference of the Parties shall make every effort to achieve consensus on each amendment. If all efforts at consensus have been exhausted and no agreement has been reached, the amendment shall, as a last resort, require for its adoption a two-thirds majority vote of the States Parties to this Protocol present and voting at the meeting of the Conference of the Parties.

2. Regional economic integration organizations, in matters within their competence, shall exercise their right to vote under this article with a number of votes equal to the number of their member States that are Parties to this Protocol. Such organizations shall not exercise their right to vote if their member States exercise theirs and *vice versa*.

3. An amendment adopted in accordance with paragraph 1 of

this article is subject to ratification, acceptance or approval by States Parties.

4. An amendment adopted in accordance with paragraph 1 of this article shall enter into force in respect of a State Party ninety days after the date of the deposit with the Secretary-General of the United Nations of an instrument of ratification, acceptance or approval of such amendment.

5. When an amendment enters into force, it shall be binding on those States Parties which have expressed their consent to be bound by it. Other States Parties shall still be bound by the provisions of this Protocol and any earlier amendments that they have ratified, accepted or approved.

Article 19. Denunciation

1. A State Party may denounce this Protocol by written notification to the Secretary-General of the United Nations. Such denunciation shall become effective one year after the date of receipt of the notification by the Secretary-General.

2. A regional economic integration organization shall cease to be a Party to this Protocol when all of its member States have denounced it.

Article 20. Depositary and languages

1. The Secretary-General of the United Nations is designated depositary of this Protocol.

2. The original of this Protocol, of which the Arabic, Chinese, English, French, Russian and Spanish texts are equally authentic, shall be deposited with the Secretary-General of the United Nations.

IN WITNESS WHEREOF, the undersigned plenipotentiaries, being duly authorized thereto by their respective Governments, have signed this Protocol.

Annexure 4

Optional Protocol to the Convention on the Rights of the Child on the Sale of Children, Child Prostitution and Child Pornography

The States Parties to the present Protocol,

Considering that, in order further to achieve the purposes of the Convention on the Rights of the Child and the implementation of its provisions, especially articles 1, 11, 21, 32, 33, 34, 35 and 36, it would be appropriate to extend the measures that States Parties should undertake in order to guarantee the protection of the child from the sale of children, child prostitution and child pornography,

Considering also that the Convention on the Rights of the Child recognizes the right of the child to be protected from economic exploitation and from performing any work that is likely to be hazardous or to interfere with the child's education, or to be harmful to the child's health or physical, mental, spiritual, moral or social development,

Gravely concerned at the significant and increasing international traffic of children for the purpose of the sale of children, child prostitution and child pornography,

Deeply concerned at the widespread and continuing practice of sex tourism, to which children are especially vulnerable, as it directly promotes the sale of children, child prostitution and child pornography,

Recognizing that a number of particularly vulnerable groups, including girl children, are at greater risk of sexual exploitation, and that girl children are disproportionately represented among the sexually exploited,

Concerned about the growing availability of child pornography on the Internet and other evolving technologies, and recalling the International Conference on Combating Child Pornography on the Internet (Vienna, 1999) and, in particular, its conclusion calling for the worldwide criminalization of the production, distribution, exportation, transmission, importation, intentional possession and advertising of child pornography, and stressing the importance of closer cooperation and partnership between Governments and the

Internet industry,

Believing that the elimination of the sale of children, child prostitution and child pornography will be facilitated by adopting a holistic approach, addressing the contributing factors, including underdevelopment, poverty, economic disparities, inequitable socio-economic structure, dysfunctioning families, lack of education, urban-rural migration, gender discrimination, irresponsible adult sexual behaviour, harmful traditional practices, armed conflicts and trafficking of children,

Believing that efforts to raise public awareness are needed to reduce consumer demand for the sale of children, child prostitution and child pornography, and also believing in the importance of strengthening global partnership among all actors and of improving law enforcement at the national level,

Noting the provisions of international legal instruments relevant to the protection of children, including the Hague Convention on the Protection of Children and Cooperation with Respect to Inter-Country Adoption, the Hague Convention on the Civil Aspects of International Child Abduction, the Hague Convention on Jurisdiction, Applicable Law, Recognition, Enforcement and Cooperation in Respect of Parental Responsibility and Measures for the Protection of Children, and International Labour Organization Convention No. 182 on the Prohibition and Immediate Action for the Elimination of the Worst Forms of Child Labour,

Encouraged by the overwhelming support for the Convention on the Rights of the Child, demonstrating the widespread commitment that exists for the promotion and protection of the rights of the child,

Recognizing the importance of the implementation of the provisions of the Programme of Action for the Prevention of the Sale of Children, Child Prostitution and Child Pornography and the Declaration and Agenda for Action adopted at the World Congress against Commercial Sexual Exploitation of Children, held at Stockholm from 27 to 31 August 1996, and the other relevant decisions and recommendations of pertinent international bodies,

Taking due account of the importance of the traditions and cultural values of each people for the protection and harmonious development of the child,

Have agreed as follows:

Article 1

States Parties shall prohibit the sale of children, child prostitution and child pornography as provided for by the present Protocol.

Article 2

For the purpose of the present Protocol:

(a) Sale of children means any act or transaction whereby a child is transferred by any person or group of persons to another for remuneration or any other consideration;

(b) Child prostitution means the use of a child in sexual activities for remuneration or any other form of consideration;

(c) Child pornography means any representation, by whatever means, of a child engaged in real or simulated explicit sexual activities or any representation of the sexual parts of a child for primarily sexual purposes.

Article 3

1. Each State Party shall ensure that, as a minimum, the following acts and activities are fully covered under its criminal or penal law, whether these offences are committed domestically or transnationally or on an individual or organized basis:

(a) In the context of sale of children as defined in article 2:

  (i) The offering, delivering or accepting, by whatever means, a child for the purpose of:

    a. Sexual exploitation of the child;

    b. Transfer of organs of the child for profit;

    c. Engagement of the child in forced labour;

  (ii) Improperly inducing consent, as an intermediary, for the adoption of a child in violation of applicable international legal instruments on adoption;

(b) Offering, obtaining, procuring or providing a child for child prostitution, as defined in article 2;

(c) Producing, distributing, disseminating, importing, exporting, offering, selling or possessing for the above purposes child pornography as defined in article 2.

2. Subject to the provisions of a State Party's national law, the

same shall apply to an attempt to commit any of these acts and to complicity or participation in any of these acts.

3. Each State Party shall make these offences punishable by appropriate penalties that take into account their grave nature.

4. Subject to the provisions of its national law, each State Party shall take measures, where appropriate, to establish the liability of legal persons for offences established in paragraph 1 of the present article. Subject to the legal principles of the State Party, this liability of legal persons may be criminal, civil or administrative.

5. States Parties shall take all appropriate legal and administrative measures to ensure that all persons involved in the adoption of a child act in conformity with applicable international legal instruments.

Article 4

1. Each State Party shall take such measures as may be necessary to establish its jurisdiction over the offences referred to in article 3, paragraph 1, when the offences are committed in its territory or on board a ship or aircraft registered in that State.

2. Each State Party may take such measures as may be necessary to establish its jurisdiction over the offences referred to in article 3, paragraph 1, in the following cases:

(a) When the alleged offender is a national of that State or a person who has his habitual residence in its territory;

(b) When the victim is a national of that State.

3. Each State Party shall also take such measures as may be necessary to establish its jurisdiction over the above-mentioned offences when the alleged offender is present in its territory and it does not extradite him or her to another State Party on the ground that the offence has been committed by one of its nationals.

4. This Protocol does not exclude any criminal jurisdiction exercised in accordance with internal law.

Article 5

1. The offences referred to in article 3, paragraph 1, shall be deemed to be included as extraditable offences in any extradition treaty existing between States Parties and shall be included as

extraditable offences in every extradition treaty subsequently concluded between them, in accordance with the conditions set forth in those treaties.

2. If a State Party that makes extradition conditional on the existence of a treaty receives a request for extradition from another State Party with which it has no extradition treaty, it may consider this Protocol as a legal basis for extradition in respect of such offences. Extradition shall be subject to the conditions provided by the law of the requested State.

3. States Parties that do not make extradition conditional on the existence of a treaty shall recognize such offences as extraditable offences between themselves subject to the conditions provided by the law of the requested State.

4. Such offences shall be treated, for the purpose of extradition between States Parties, as if they had been committed not only in the place in which they occurred but also in the territories of the States required to establish their jurisdiction in accordance with article 4.

5. If an extradition request is made with respect to an offence described in article 3, paragraph 1, and if the requested State Party does not or will not extradite on the basis of the nationality of the offender, that State shall take suitable measures to submit the case to its competent authorities for the purpose of prosecution.

Article 6

1. States Parties shall afford one another the greatest measure of assistance in connection with investigations or criminal or extradition proceedings brought in respect of the offences set forth in article 3, paragraph 1, including assistance in obtaining evidence at their disposal necessary for the proceedings.

2. States Parties shall carry out their obligations under paragraph 1 of the present article in conformity with any treaties or other arrangements on mutual legal assistance that may exist between them. In the absence of such treaties or arrangements, States Parties shall afford one another assistance in accordance with their domestic law.

Article 7

States Parties shall, subject to the provisions of their national law:

(a) Take measures to provide for the seizure and confiscation, as appropriate, of:

(i) Goods such as materials, assets and other instrumentalities used to commit or facilitate offences under the present Protocol;

(ii) Proceeds derived from such offences;

(b) Execute requests from another State Party for seizure or confiscation of goods or proceeds referred to in subparagraph (a) (i);

(c) Take measures aimed at closing, on a temporary or definitive basis, premises used to commit such offences.

Articles 8

1. States Parties shall adopt appropriate measures to protect the rights and interests of child victims of the practices prohibited under the present Protocol at all stages of the criminal justice process, in particular by:

(a) Recognising the vulnerability of child victims and adapting procedures to recognize their special needs, including their special needs as witnesses;

(b) Informing child victims of their rights, their role and the scope, timing and progress of the proceedings and of the disposition of their cases;

(c) Allowing the views, needs and concerns of child victims to be presented and considered in proceedings where their personal interests are affected, in a manner consistent with the procedural rules of national law;

(d) Providing appropriate support services to child victims throughout the legal process;

(e) Protecting, as appropriate, the privacy and identity of child victims and taking measures in accordance with national law to avoid the inappropriate dissemination of information that could lead to the identification of child victims;

(f) Providing, in appropriate cases, for the safety of child victims, as well as that of their families and witnesses on their behalf, from intimidation and retaliation;

(g) Avoiding unnecessary delay in the disposition of cases and the execution of orders or decrees granting compensation to child victims.

2. States Parties shall ensure that uncertainty as to the actual age of the victim shall not prevent the initiation of criminal investigations, including investigations aimed at establishing the age of the victim.

3. States Parties shall ensure that, in the treatment by the criminal justice system of children who are victims of the offences described in the present Protocol, the best interest of the child shall be a primary consideration.

4. States Parties shall take measures to ensure appropriate training, in particular legal and psychological training, for the persons who work with victims of the offences prohibited under the present Protocol.

5. States Parties shall, in appropriate cases, adopt measures in order to protect the safety and integrity of those persons and/or organizations involved in the prevention and/or protection and rehabilitation of victims of such offences.

6. Nothing in the present article shall be construed as prejudicial to or inconsistent with the rights of the accused to a fair and impartial trial.

Article 9

1. States Parties shall adopt or strengthen, implement and disseminate laws, administrative measures, social policies and programmes to prevent the offences referred to in the present Protocol. Particular attention shall be given to protect children who arc especially vulnerable to these practices.

2. States Parties shall promote awareness in the public at large, including children, through information by all appropriate means, education and training, about the preventive measures and harmful effects of the offences referred to in the present Protocol. In fulfilling their obligations under this article, States Parties shall encourage the participation of the community and, in particular, children and child victims, in such information and education and training programmes, including at the international level.

3. States Parties shall take all feasible measures with the aim of ensuring all appropriate assistance to victims of such offences,

including their full social reintegration and their full physical and psychological recovery.

4. States Parties shall ensure that all child victims of the offences described in the present Protocol have access to adequate procedures to seek, without discrimination, compensation for damages from those legally responsible.

5. States Parties shall take appropriate measures aimed at effectively prohibiting the production and dissemination of material advertising the offences described in the present Protocol.

Article 10

1. States Parties shall take all necessary steps to strengthen international cooperation by multilateral, regional and bilateral arrangements for the prevention, detection, investigation, prosecution and punishment of those responsible for acts involving the sale of children, child prostitution, child pornography and child sex tourism. States Parties shall also promote international cooperation and coordination between their authorities, national and international non-governmental organizations and international organizations.

2. States Parties shall promote international cooperation to assist child victims in their physical and psychological recovery, social reintegration and repatriation.

3. States Parties shall promote the strengthening of international cooperation in order to address the root causes, such as poverty and underdevelopment, contributing to the vulnerability of children to the sale of children, child prostitution, child pornography and child sex tourism.

4. States Parties in a position to do so shall provide financial, technical or other assistance through existing multilateral, regional, bilateral or other programmes.

Article 11

Nothing in the present Protocol shall affect any provisions that are more conducive to the realization of the rights of the child and that may be contained in:

(a) The law of a State Party;

(b) International law in force for that State.

Article 12

1. Each State Party shall submit, within two years following the entry into force of the Protocol for that State Party, a report to the Committee on the Rights of the Child providing comprehensive information on the measures it has taken to implement the provisions of the Protocol.

2. Following the submission of the comprehensive report, each State Party shall include in the reports they submit to the Committee on the Rights of the Child, in accordance with article 44 of the Convention, any further information with respect to the implementation of the Protocol. Other States Parties to the Protocol shall submit a report every five years.

3. The Committee on the Rights of the Child may request from States Parties further information relevant to the implementation of this Protocol.

Article 13

1. The present Protocol is open for signature by any State that is a party to the Convention or has signed it.

2. The present Protocol is subject to ratification and is open to accession by any State that is a party to the Convention or has signed it. Instruments of ratification or accession shall be deposited with the Secretary-General of the United Nations.

Article 14

1. The present Protocol shall enter into force three months after the deposit of the tenth instrument of ratification or accession.

2. For each State ratifying the present Protocol or acceding to it after its entry into force, the present Protocol shall enter into force one month after the date of the deposit of its own instrument of ratification or accession.

Article 15

1. Any State Party may denounce the present Protocol at any time by written notification to the Secretary-General of the United Nations, who shall thereafter inform the other States Parties to the

Convention and all States that have signed the Convention. The denunciation shall take effect one year after the date of receipt of the notification by the Secretary-General of the United Nations.

2. Such a denunciation shall not have the effect of releasing the State Party from its obligations under this Protocol in regard to any offence that occurs prior to the date on which the denunciation becomes effective. Nor shall such a denunciation prejudice in any way the continued consideration of any matter that is already under consideration by the Committee prior to the date on which the denunciation becomes effective.

Article 16

1. Any State Party may propose an amendment and file it with the Secretary-General of the United Nations. The Secretary-General shall thereupon communicate the proposed amendment to States Parties, with a request that they indicate whether they favour a conference of States Parties for the purpose of considering and voting upon the proposals. In the event that, within four months from the date of such communication, at least one-third of the States Parties favour such a conference, the Secretary-General shall convene the conference under the auspices of the United Nations. Any amendment adopted by a majority of States Parties present and voting at the conference shall be submitted to the General Assembly for approval.

2. An amendment adopted in accordance with paragraph 1 of the present article shall enter into force when it has been approved by the General Assembly of the United Nations and accepted by a two-thirds majority of States Parties.

3. When an amendment enters into force, it shall be binding on those States Parties that have accepted it, other States Parties still being bound by the provisions of the present Protocol and any earlier amendments that they have accepted.

Article 17

1. The present Protocol, of which the Arabic, Chinese, English, French, Russian and Spanish texts are equally authentic, shall be deposited in the archives of the United Nations.

2. The Secretary-General of the United Nations shall transmit

certified copies of the present Protocol to all States Parties to the Convention and all States that have signed the Convention.

Notes

1. United Nations, *Treaty Series*, vol. 189, No. 2545.
2. *Ibid.*, Vol. 606, No. 8791.

Bibliography

AIR 1990 SC 1412.

AIR 1997 SC 3021.

Benjamin N. Cardozo, *The Nature of the Judicial Process*, Universal Law Publishing, Delhi, Eighth Indian Reprint 2010, p. 83.

Bhattacharjee, S. (2016, April 16). *Why is Meghalaya Vulnerable Towards Crime of Human Trafficking?*. Retrieved January 8, 2017, from neLive: http://www.nelive.in/meghalaya/opinion/whymeghalayavulnerable-towardscrimehumantrafficking.

Dhananjay Mahapatra (2010). Missionaries trafficking kids from NE states? *The Times of India*, Pune.

Dina Siegel and Sylvia de Blank, "*Women who traffic women: the role of women in human trafficking networks – Dutch cases*", Global Crime (Routledge) 11, no. 4 (November 2010): 436-447.

Gabhan, S.N. (2006). Human Trafficking: A Twenty-First Century Slavery. *The Furrow, 57* (10), 528-537.

Ghosh, A.K. (n.d.). *Child Rights to Protection in Manipur Context*. Retrieved October 10, 2016, from CRY - Child Rights and You.

Ghosh, Biswajit. "Trafficking in women and children in India: nature, dimensions and strategies for prevention." *The International Journal of Human Rights* (Routledge) 13, no. 5 (December 2009): 716–738.

Government of India, Ministry of Home Affairs, Centre State Division, Dated, 25th June, 2013.

Hannah. G. *et al. India's Human Trafficking Laws and Policies and the UN Trafficking Protocol: Achieving Clarity*. Kolkata: Jindal Global Law School.

James Khagenbam (2012). *Child Trafficking: Many rescued yet dozens of minor traceless since 2010* (three Parts).

Kamier, T.L. (2015). *Indigenous Women and Human Trakkicking in the Mekong Region: Policy Overview and Community Response*. Chiang Mai: Asia Indigenous Peoples Pact (AIPP).

Kapur, Kirti Singh and Diviya. "Law, Violence, and the Girl Child." *Health and Human Rights* 5, no. 2 (2001): 8-29.

Khan, I. (n.d.). *Child Trafficking in India: A Concern*. Retrieved November 17, 2016.

Kumar, A. (2015). *Status of Child Trafficking and Laws Related to It*. National Law University and Judicial Academy, Assam. Guwahati: NCPCR.

Manipur Women Gun Survivors Network. (2016). *NE RECORDS HIGHEST EVER 1,539 TRAFFICKING CASES IN 2015*. New Delhi: Manipur Women Gun Survivors Network.

Ministry of Home Affairs and Ministry of External Affairs, Government of India (Compiled by authors from the websites).

Ministry of Home Affairs, Government of India, 2015-2016, pp. 71-72.

Nagaland State Social Welfare Board. (2013). *Consultative Meeting on Combating Human Trafficking in Nagaland*. Kohima: The Nagaland State Social Welfare Board.

National Commission for Protection of Child Rights (No Date), Concept Note: *A Regional Consultation on Child Trafficking from and into 8 North Eastern States of India 2014-15*.

Niumai, A. (2016). Unspoken Voices of Trafficked Women and Children in Manipur. *Economic & Political Weekly, LI* (44 & 45), 69-76.

Order No. 16/10/2010-S(SW) dt. the 2nd November, 2010, Department of Social Welfare, Government of Manipur.

Order No. 2/11/(1A)/2009-H, dt. the 4th March, 2011, Department of Home, Government of Manipur.

Order No. 9/14/2010-SW (JJA) dt. 5th April, 2010, Department of Social Welfare, Government of India.

Order No. 9/25/2009-S (SW) dt. the 15th October, 2011, Department of Social Welfare, Government of Manipur.

Order No. 9/26/2009-S (SW) pt. dt. 7/4/2010, Department of Social Welfare, Government of Manipur.

Paresh. (2015). *A Regional Consultation on Child Trafficking from and into 8 North Eastern States of India 2014-15*. National Commission for Protection of Child Rights, Government of India, North East Cell. New Delhi: NCPCR.

Press Information Bureau, Ministry of Home Affairs (2015). Shri Rajnath Singh inaugurates National Conference on Anti-Human Trafficking, 07-October.

Sapam Dilipkumar, *Child Rights in Manipur*, Waba Publications, Imphal, 2016, p. 100.

Sarkar, Siddhartha. "Rethinking Human Trafficking in India: Nature, Extent and Identification of Survivors." *The Round Table* (Routledge) 103, no. 5 (2014): 483–495.

Section 30 of the JJ Act, 2015.

Síle Nic Gabhan, "Human Trafficking: A Twenty-First Century Slavery", *The Furrow* 57, no. 10 (2006): 528-537.

Smriti Rao and Christina Presenti, "Understanding Human Trafficking Origin: A Cross-Country Empirical Analysis", *Feminist Economics* 18, no. 2 (2012): 231-263.

The Sangai Express (July 31, 2012, August 08, 2012 October 07, 2012).

Uddin, M. Bashir. "Human Trafficking in South Asia: Issues of Corruption and Human Security." *International Journal of Social Work and Human Services Practice* 2, no. 1 (Feb 2014): 18-27.

United Nations Office on Drugs and Crime, *Global Report on Trafficking in Persons 2014*, Annual Report (New York: United Nations, 2014).

Index